BOOKS inBLOOM

Valerie Bang-Jensen &
Mark Lubkowitz

Published by the National Gardening Association
Williston, Vermont

The Teaching Gardens of Saint Michael's College

One Winooski Park, Colchester, Vermont, USA 05439

802.654.2000 • Academics.SMCVT.edu/Gardens/Home.html

We'd like to thank Saint Michael's College for supporting our vision, Alan Dickinson for his knowledge and gentle guidance, and Ginger and Lars for their willingness to play along through their unwavering indulgence.

National Gardening Association

237 Commerce Street, Suite 101, Williston, Vermont 05495

802-863-5251 • Garden.org • KidsGardening.org

As a national nonprofit leader in plant-based education based in Williston, Vermont, the National Gardening Association's (NGA) mission is to empower every generation to lead healthier lives, build stronger communities, and encourage environmental stewardship through educational gardening programs. Our award-winning websites (**Garden.org**, **KidsGardening.org**, and **GardeningWithKids.org**), e-newsletters, online courses, grants and awards, curricula for youth gardening, and research for the lawn and garden industry are widely respected resources for educators and gardeners alike.

PROJECT STAFF

AUTHORS: Valerie Bang-Jensen & Mark Lubkowitz   DESIGN: Jessica Hill

EDITOR: Sarah Pounders   ILLUSTRATIONS: Suzanne LeGault

ISBN-13: 978-0-615-93680-2

ISBN-10: 0615936806

Library of Congress Control Number: 2014931828

Why This Book?

We wrote *Books in Bloom* because great books can help young children learn about science while experiencing a good story. Our collection includes outstanding picture books that are widely recognized as good literature and that discuss or reference plant biology. The importance of gardening, farming, and plants in our everyday lives is revealed in *Books in Bloom*, which provides an opportunity for anyone who reads and gardens with children to teach science through literature.

Just as *The Wonderful Wizard of Oz* may have taught you that poppies can put people to sleep, the books featured in *Books in Bloom* can help teach the children in your life about botany through literature. *Tell Me, Tree*, for example, delves into leaf shapes and unlocks the mysteries of photosynthesis. *Compost Stew* rhymes its way through the wonders of rotting matter and reveals the importance of soil nutrients to plants. *The Gardener* examines the power of flowers and gardening in coping with human hardship during the Great Depression. We explore genre, themes, nonfiction features, and plant biology as they occur authentically in each of the books we have chosen to share with you.

We hope you will have as much fun exploring the books and engaging your young readers in the gardening activities as we did writing them!

How to Use This Book

Quick Reference

Each chapter provides a series of quick reference icons which identify the appropriate grade levels for the included lesson plans.

Anyone interested in a good read, picture books, or gardening will find a wealth of information in these chapters and lots of jumping-off points for getting his or her hands dirty. Whether in the form of a compelling read-aloud or advice about starting a garden, *Books in Bloom* will provide families, classrooms, and after-school and library programs with endless opportunities to learn about people, plants, and gardens. Each chapter features one picture book and can be used on its own or combined with others to make a more comprehensive unit, or even an entire standards-based curriculum.

Each chapter consists of the sections below.

 Why We Love This Book describes the unique features that appeal to us.

 Discover the Book presents a synopsis of both the story and the plant biology and describes literary elements found in both fiction and nonfiction, which might include text structure, access features, plot, setting, and writing and illustration styles.

 Explore the Biology explains the key biological concepts in an accessible way, revealing the biological backstory through use of background information, examples, and illustrations.

 Digging Deeper

Talking Points are questions to ask readers to draw out the literary themes and biological concepts in the book. A starting point for discussion is provided for each question.

Learning Experiences are compact lessons and activities that help you extend the biological, artistic, and literary concepts of the book in a hands-on manner. In each chapter, one of the learning experiences is expanded into a full lesson plan provided in a separate section.

Common Core

Connections to the Common Core State Standards and Next Generation Science Standards are provided in tables on pages 121 and 123.

 Related Books are other titles that could replace the featured book or that provide additional information, or books at an alternative reading level.

 The **Lesson Plan** presents an expanded version of one of the learning experiences, including teaching materials and detailed instructions.

Books In Bloom: How to Use This Book

Table of Contents

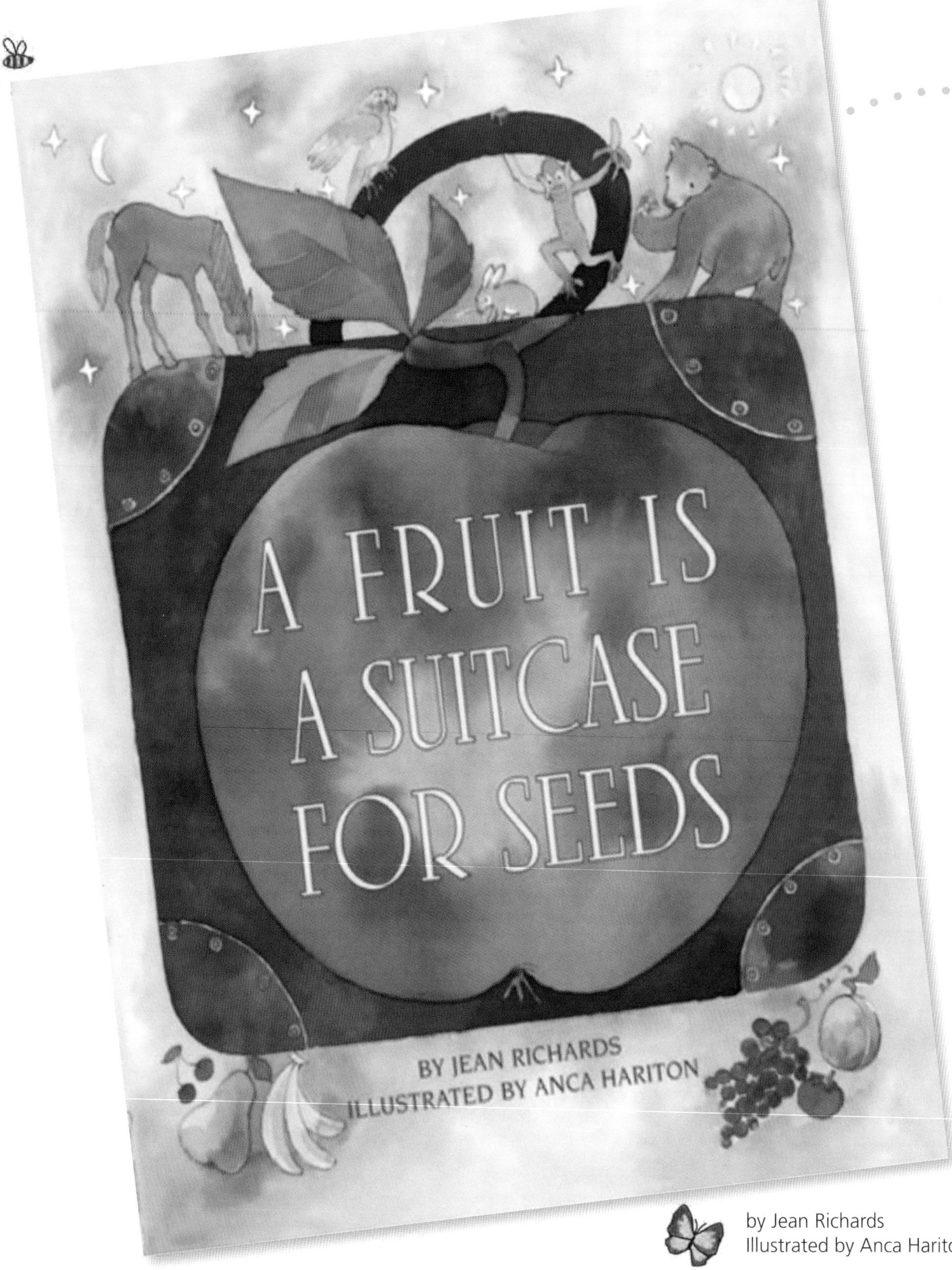

A FRUIT IS A SUITCASE FOR SEEDS

BY JEAN RICHARDS
ILLUSTRATED BY ANCA HARITON

by Jean Richards
Illustrated by Anca Hariton

The Millbrook Press (2002)
Grade Level: K-2

A Fruit is a Suitcase for Seeds

What We Love About This Book

- Strong metaphor that works
- Humorous illustrations

Discover the Book

In this nonfiction book, the text and watercolor illustrations work together to help young readers understand the concept of seed dispersal, and how fruit is like a suitcase, offering covering and protection while facilitating travel. Children will enjoy the continuous panel running along the bottom of the pages that presents stylized interpretations of each concept. For example, where the text says "some seeds travel in water," the main illustration shows a branch with fruit floating down a stream, and the cartoonish figure at the bottom is paddling a boat with a suitcase aboard. Humorous visual details, such as earrings fashioned out of cherries and suitcases filled with seeds, abound.

Explore the Biology

Discussing fruit is one of our favorite classroom conversations because fruit is such a commonly misused botanical word. In the vernacular, the definition of fruit is highly inconsistent. We all recognize oranges, apples, and bananas as fruits because they are edible, sweet, fleshy, and sold in the grocery store, but we do not typically refer to squash and tomatoes as fruits even though they are. Botanically, fruit develops from the flower and thus encases the plant's seeds. More specifically, fruit can be divided into two categories: true fruit, which is derived from the floral ovary, and accessory fruit, which develops from other parts of the flower. No matter how it developed, you can always recognize a fruit if it contains seeds, although the fruit is sometimes not obvious. For example, when children blow on a dandelion, as shown in the first few pages, it is the light and wispy fruit that carries the seeds away. Even less apparent are the fruits that surround grass seeds, as exemplified by the outer "skin" of the corn kernel.

The title of this book, *A Fruit Is a Suitcase for Seeds*, accurately captures the main idea of the text: the purpose of fruit is to protect and distribute seeds. The author begins by introducing the role of seeds in propagation and then quickly segues to the different ways that fruit can spread seeds. A key concept in biology is that form and function are related (which is why you never see a watermelon blowing in the wind), and throughout the text this idea is reinforced by illustrations showing how various types of fruit disperse seeds. Seeds are spread by wind, water, or even animals such as monkeys, bats, and parrots, which "poop seeds" after eating the fruit. Readers may be interested in learning of two additional mechanisms not mentioned: hitchhiking seeds, like burrs, stick to the fur of animals, and some plants can shoot their seeds using a fruit that dries under tension (such as lupines, impatiens, and witch hazel).

Digging Deeper

Talking Points

1. **Why is a suitcase used as a metaphor for fruit?**

   A metaphor helps us make comparisons by using one concept to illuminate another. Ask readers to provide several reasons that a suitcase is a useful metaphor for fruit. They may consider: travel and protection. To extend this idea, they might think of metaphors for specific fruits.

2. **Why are there so many different types of fruit?**

   The central theme of this book is that fruits help plants disperse their seeds by co-opting help from wind, water, and animals. Use this question to emphasize that form and function are related. Go through the text and make a table of the different fruits presented and identify which use wind, water, or animals to carry their seeds.

3. **Why is it important for seeds to travel?**

   What would happen if seeds were all dropped in the same place? The strongest explanation will include the idea that seeds (siblings) and parents compete for nutrients and space.

Strawberry Flowers Form True and Accessory Fruit

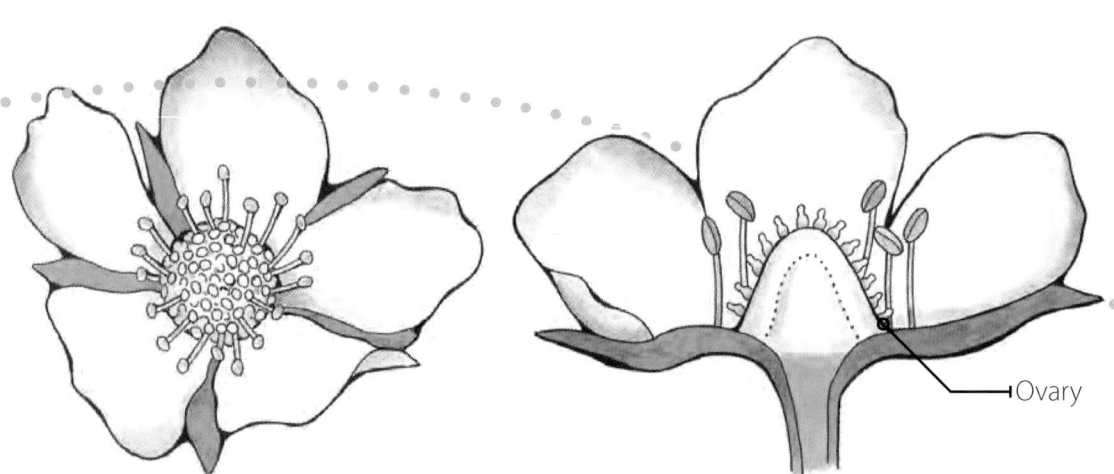

Ovary

Learning Experiences

1. Classify fruits and vegetables.

Fruits come in many shapes and sizes, and they are not always easy to identify. Adding to the confusion, many fruits, such as tomatoes and zucchini, are commonly labeled vegetables. Ask your readers if tomatoes, squash, peppers, cucumbers, eggplants, and peas are fruits or vegetables. Many will consider them vegetables, but as the text reveals, they are really fruits. Ask your readers to define "fruit" and "vegetable." Vegetables are leaves, roots, or stems; anything that contains a seed is a fruit. Make a list of "vegetables" with your readers and have them identify which are really fruits. True vegetables include carrots, cabbage, broccoli, cauliflower, parsnips, celery, and spinach. Common fruits that are called vegetables include tomatoes, squash, pumpkins, cucumbers, and peppers.

2. Make fruit prints.

Cut fruit in half, dip the pieces in paint, and stamp the impressions on paper. This makes a perfect permanent cross-section for future comparison and study (as opposed to using the real fruit, which will unfortunately decompose). Possible extensions include labeling parts of the fruit, grouping prints by type of fruit or type of seed dispersal, and creating mathematical statements or questions (how many sections do you see in this grapefruit?). A fruit print mural or collage makes fine wrapping paper or bulletin board backdrops.

3. Design your own fruit.

As a way to help learners apply their new understanding about the role of fruit in seed dispersal, challenge them to create their own fruit. Begin by having them choose a strategy to distribute their seeds and then design a fruit to translocate the seeds from the parent plant to some other location. Some questions for them to consider: what will they use as their agent (wind, water, animal, or plant), how far should the seeds travel, and is their design consistent with the plant's strategy for survival (for example, aquatic plants need to ensure that their seeds land in water)? Ask them to consider what the seeds would look like. Younger children could adapt this activity by acting out different agents carrying fruit.

Related Texts

A Seed is Sleepy
By Dianna Hutts Aston
Illustrated by Sylvia Long

Chronicle Books (2007)
Grade Level: K-5

. . . .

Plant Secrets (p.63)
By Emily Goodman
Illustrated by Phyllis Limbacher Tildes

Published by Charlesbridge (2009)
Grade Level: K-2

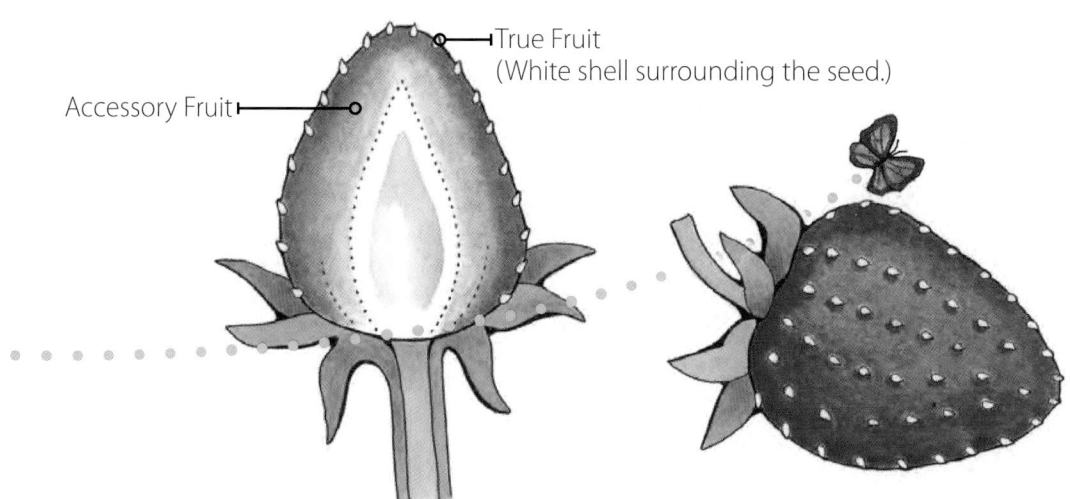

Accessory Fruit

True Fruit
(White shell surrounding the seed.)

Design a New Fruit

Objective	To demonstrate an understanding of seed dispersal by designing a new fruit.
Time	1 hour
Materials	• Various craft supplies such as construction paper, scissors, glue, chenille sticks, feathers, and beads • Table of Seed Transportation
Laying the Groundwork	Ask readers: • What would happen if all the seeds a plant made dropped to the ground and started to grow? (The new plants would compete for water, nutrients, light, and space.) • Since they don't have legs, how do seeds move away from their parent plant? (The fruit of the plant is designed to help them move via wind or water, or to entice animals to carry them away.)
Exploration	1. Explain to readers the different ways that fruits help move seeds and bring in examples of each method. Use the Table of Seed Transportation as background information. 2. Have readers make their own fruit and seeds using craft supplies. They can work on their own or in a group. Instruct them to first decide how they want the seeds to travel, and then create a fruit to be the "suitcase" for their seeds. Ask them to come up with a name for their fruit. 3. After they complete their creation, give them the opportunity to share.

Branching Out

Have readers create a short story or picture book detailing how their new fruit moves from the parent plant to a new location.

Fruit and Seeds from Common Foods

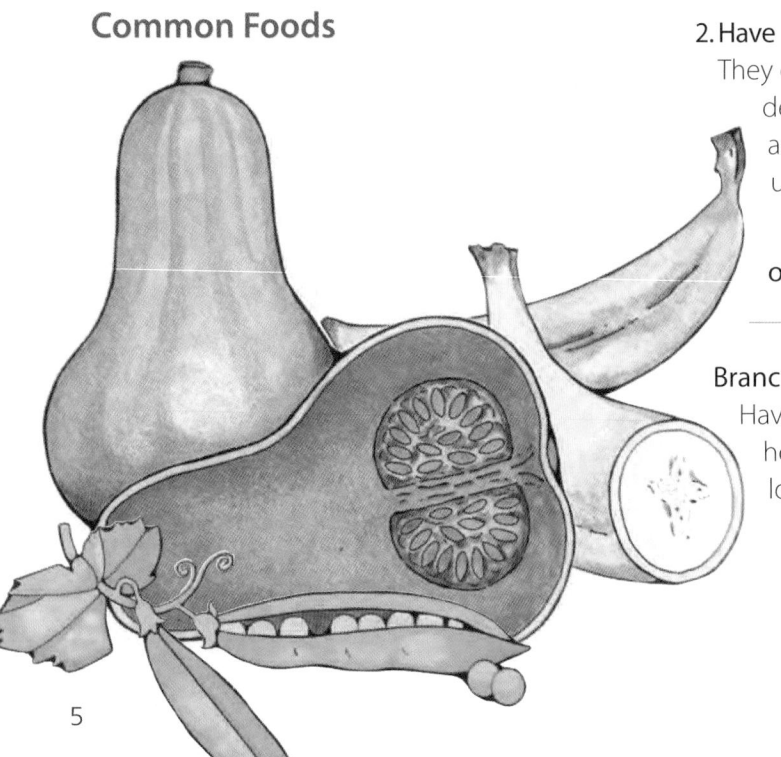

NAME   DATE

Table of Seed Transportation

Method of Travel	Fruit Characteristics	Example
Wind	Fruits are light and have a large surface-area-to-volume ratio in order to sail or parachute on the wind.	
Water	Fruits are buoyant.	
Animal	Edible fruits, when ripe, tend to be sweet tasting and smelling as well as highly visible. Some seeds are consumed and dispersed in scat (e.g. tomato) while others are not (e.g peach pit).	
Hitchhiker Fruits	Fruit has Velcro-like extensions that are used for attachment.	

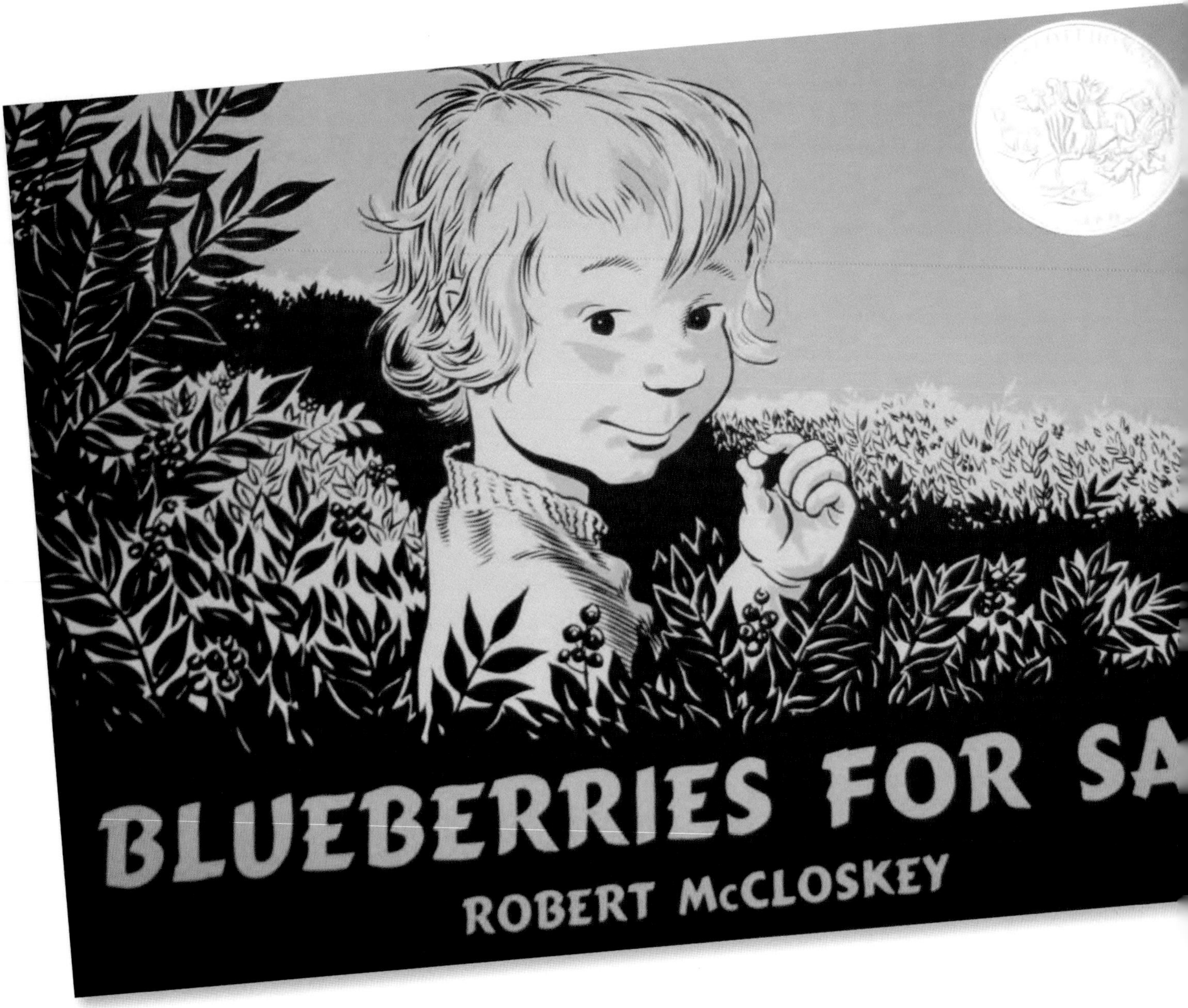

BLUEBERRIES FOR SA

ROBERT McCLOSKEY

Written & illustrated by
Robert McCloskey

Viking Press (1948)
Grade Level: K-1

Blueberries for Sal

 What We Love About This Book

- The deep blueberry ink
- The classic lost child story
- Foraging

Discover the Book

The deep blueberry ink of this book sets the tone for a day of berry-picking on Blueberry Hill. Little Sal and her mother turn to the blueberry shrubs to collect berries for making preserves to eat during the winter. In a parallel hike, Mother Bear and Little Bear are eating their way up the hill to "store up food for the long, cold winter." Robert McCloskey, the Caldecott Award–winning author/illustrator, builds child-scale tension as the mother/child pairs are separated but ultimately reunited. Though the story was first published in 1948, the experience of temporary separation is universal and will resonate with current readers.

At the beginning of the day, the two pairs collect blueberries on opposite sides of the mountain; both Little Sal and Little Bear get tired and decide to take a break. When they resume their berry-picking/eating adventure, they inadvertently match up with the wrong mother — little Sal follows the mother bear while the cub follows Little Sal's mother. Readers will be amused by the role played by crows and partridges in a case of mistaken identity as Little Sal and Little Bear search for their own parents. Each pair is eventually reunited as both human and ursine mothers recognize the unique berry-picking style of each offspring. Sal's picking makes a distinct onomatopoeic "kerplink, kerplank, kerplunk" as she fills her bucket, and Little Bear makes his presence known by spilling the berries from Sal's mother's bucket. The double-page-spread illustrations convey the openness of the Maine hills, and their size makes the book a good choice to share by reading aloud with a group. Astute readers will enjoy learning about this slice of rural life in the 1940s, and will glean information about the process of canning berries from the illustrations in the detailed end pages.

Explore the Biology

As the title implies, the blueberry gets equal billing, and is unquestionably the main botanical character of this story. The blueberry, a native perennial shrub, is found widely throughout North America and is consumed by humans and wildlife alike. The wild variety, pictured in the book, grows as a small shrub and is often called low bush; domesticated varieties are bigger plants with larger berries and called high bush. The blueberry has been termed a "superfood" for its high antioxidant levels (antioxidants are substances that protect cells from harmful chemical reactions) and for its low glycemic index (a measure of a food's impact on blood sugar levels when consumed).

In this book, the parallel between the adventures of Little Sal and her mother on Blueberry Hill and the bears' adventures extends to the biological realm as well. Both pairs of mother and offspring are foraging for winter food, but in different ways; the bears consume large quantities of blueberries and store the calories as fat to prepare for hibernation; the McCloskey family preserves the blueberries in jars, as shown in the delightfully blue end-page illustrations. The time-honored tradition of foraging is still practiced in many places in the U.S. with such foods as blackberries, raspberries, and blueberries.

Digging Deeper

Talking Points

1. How do you gather food for the winter?

   Sal and her mother are picking berries in order to preserve them for winter. Although it may be hard for readers to imagine a time when fresh foods were not shipped across the world, not too long ago, many fruits and vegetables were available only when they were in season locally. With your readers, make a list of all the produce grown in your area and then create a calendar of when each is harvested. Ask whether they consume these foods at other times of the year. Where do they come from?

2. How do bears and people survive the winter?

   Both bears and people in this story are preparing for a New England winter; both will need food and protection from the elements. Ask readers how bears and people each meet these needs. People can store or purchase food as needed, but bears must store food on their bodies. Similarly, both bears and people need shelter from the elements; whereas humans wear more clothes and turn on the heat, bears grow thick coats and seek dens that protect them. What other differences and similarities do your readers observe in the bears and people in this story?

3. How does sound help the characters reunite?

   Sal and Little Bear get mixed up on Blueberry Hill and separated from their mothers. What clues do they use to find the right mother? What sounds tell the mothers that the right child has reappeared? Young listeners might enjoy reenacting the story of a happy reunion between the pairs.

Learning Experiences

1. **Preserve your own harvest just like Sal and her mother.**

   If possible, obtain fruits or vegetables from a local school or community garden. A field trip to a local farm is another enriching opportunity. If neither of these options is available, fresh fruits or vegetables can be purchased from a local grocery store or farmer's market. There are many ways to preserve food, including canning, freezing, and drying. Food preservation techniques are employed to slow or prevent microbes from decaying and spoiling the food. Food preservation allows you to enjoy foods beyond their harvest dates, and it is also a way to decrease waste when bountiful harvests cannot be consumed promptly.

2. **Explore hibernation.**

   Bears are true hibernators and as such need to store energy for the winter. There are many good books you can use to investigate hibernation with your readers; we especially like *Animals in Winter* by Henrietta Bancroft (HarperCollins, 1997). This book helps explore how animals hibernate or migrate in winter.

3. **Use your senses to recognize people.**

   Have some fun focusing on one sense at a time. Sal's mother recognized her "kerplink, kerplank, kerplunk." Ask your readers, "Do you think you can recognize each other by voice alone?" Take turns sitting on one side of a sheet or in circle facing outward and see whether listeners can identify who is saying "kerplink, kerplank, kerplunk."

Related Books

Jamberry
Written and Illustrated by
Bruce Degen

Published by HarperFestival (1995)
Grade Level: PreK-1

. . . .

Blueberries for the Queen
Written by Katherine and
John Paterson
Illustrated by Susan Jeffers

Published by HarperCollins (2004)
Grade Level: K-3

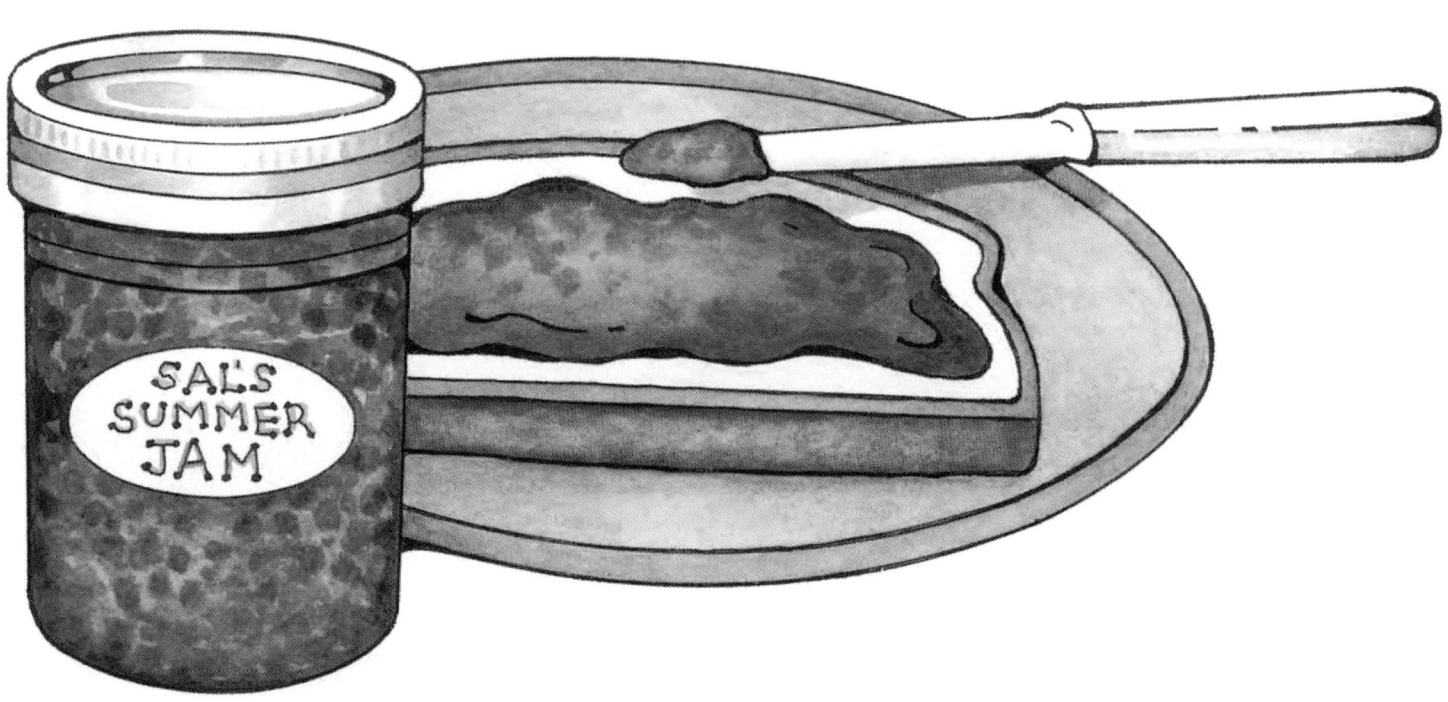

 **Lesson Plan**

Preserving Fruit

Objective	To learn why and how fresh food can be preserved for later consumption.
Time	2 or more hours
Materials	• Ingredients for making jam (see included recipe) • Cooking supplies such as bowls, spoons, and jars
Laying the Groundwork	Ask readers: • **Do the fresh fruits and vegetables available in our grocery stores grow in our area during the winter?** If no, where do they come from? (Fruits and vegetables are shipped from all over the world. This is possible because of fast transportation and technology such as refrigeration.) • **Before refrigeration, how did people preserve food?** (They used to preserve foods for later consumption using techniques like drying, smoking, and canning. People could eat fresh fruits and vegetables only when they were in season.) Introduce readers to common preservation techniques, including: • **Drying** - This prevents meat and produce from rotting and prevents stored seeds from sprouting. It also inhibits the growth of microorganisms while the food is dry. • **Heating** - Heat can increase shelf life by temporarily sterilizing food. • **Freezing** - Frozen foods remain in edible condition almost indefinitely because the low temperatures prevent microbes from growing. • **Fermentation** - Fermentation is a gradual chemical change caused by the enzymes of some bacteria, molds, and yeasts. It is used to produce bread, vinegar, cheese, sauerkraut, alcoholic beverages, and yogurt. • **Chemical preservation** - Humans have used chemical preservatives for millennia. Salt was extremely precious in ancient times, in part because it was a great preservative for meat and other foods. Smoking is another ancient and common means of chemical food preservation. Many spices are rich in compounds that slow bacterial growth or even kill bacteria. • **Irradiation** - A more recent technology, irradiation, is used to destroy microorganisms on many spices and is increasingly used on fruits, vegetables, and berries. (Readers might want to investigate different sides of the controversy surrounding irradiated foods.)

11

Books In Bloom: Blueberries for Sal

Exploration	1. Make your own jam using fruit from a school garden, a local farmer's market, or a grocery store.

If cooking in the classroom, send home a notice that includes the recipe you will make and ask parents to alert you to any food allergies. Also make sure to review the following safety tips:

– Always wash your hands before preparing food.

– Wash fruits and vegetables in running water and dry them with a clean towel.

– Use clean utensils and clean all working surfaces.

– Prepare fruits and vegetables separately from meat and poultry.
  • Work in small groups so everyone has a chance to contribute.
  • Enlist help from other teachers, parents, or community volunteers to guide and monitor the students if necessary.
  • Have enough ingredients on hand for the whole class to enjoy the results.

Here is an easy recipe to try:

Triple Berry Freezer Jam

Note: Do not alter or double the recipe as jam will not set properly.

Ingredients:
1/2 cup Blackberries
1 1/2 cup Strawberries
1 cup Blueberries
Juice of Half a Lemon
5 cup Sugar
3/4 cup Water*
1 Package Fruit Pectin*

*Pectin instructions may differ. Please refer to the instructions on your pectin package for specific water requirements.

Directions:

1. Pour blackberries, blueberries, and strawberries into large bowl and crush with potato masher .

2. Stir sugar and lemon juice into crushed berries and cover. Allow berry mixture to macerate at room temperature for 30-45 minutes (or until majority of juice has been extracted from berry mixture).

3. Add pectin to the water in a small saucepan and stir to dissolve. Bring to a boil, stirring constantly. Boil for 1 minute.

4. Stir hot pectin into berry mixture. Continue stirring for several minutes or until sugar has dissolved.

5. Pour berry pectin mixture into clean dry containers leaving about. Half inch of room at the top and cover tightly. You will have 7-8 cups of jam.

6. Leave at room temperature overnight or until jam sets.

7. Freeze jam until ready to eat (up to one year). Jam will keep in the refrigerator for up to 3 weeks.

Branching Out	Experiment with another method of food preservation. Simple projects include drying herbs or sunflowers (for the seeds) by hanging them in a dry, dark area. Another option is to construct a food dehydrator to dry fruits and vegetables like apples or tomatoes.

NAME

DATE

Design Your Jam Label

Compost Stew
An A to Z Recipe for the Earth

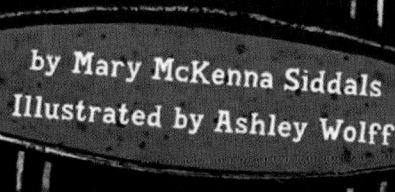

by Mary McKenna Siddals
Illustrated by Ashley Wolff

by Mary McKenna Siddals
Illustrated by Ashley Wolff

Tricycle Press (2010)
Grade Level: K-4

Compost Stew: An A-Z Recipe for the Earth

What We Love About This Book

• Rich collage illustrations
• Celebration of rotting organic material

Discover the Book

Mary McKenna Siddals and Ashley Wolff have created an ingenious alphabet book with a rhyming recipe for making compost. A group of children create "Compost Stew" by adding ingredients into the mix; apple cores (for the letter A) are followed by bruised bananas (B), and later by laundry lint (L) and teabags (T). This alphabet book passes the "Q" test with flying colors — not only is quarry dust an authentic "Q" term, but it also reflects the latest agricultural thinking about soil mineralization. Clever rhymes such as "Zinnia heads from flower beds" and "just add it to the pot and let it rot" work well linguistically and convey useful information. Even the helpful "Chef's Note" at the end uses rhyme to expand on composting. The cheery gardeners build their compost through the year, as reflected by the seasonal ingredients of autumn leaves, jack-o'-lanterns, Christmas tree needles, and old mulch, a harbinger of spring. Readers will enjoy following the participatory antics of the goose and Dalmatian on every page.

The vibrant colors and textures of the collage illustrations are captivating and entertaining. Scraps of every type of paper imaginable — textured paper, flecked paper, marbleized paper, newsprint — create an appealing three-dimensional effect. Wolff dresses the children in clothing made of photo images, newspaper, loud colors, and mixed textures that would make a hip new line of apparel. Even the dog wears a collar that is a subtle nod to the recycling theme of the book.

Explore the Biology

Many of us realize that in nature, nutrients cycle through organisms. This book uses alphabet and rhyme to showcase how common organic material can be composted. Composting is the practice of collecting and managing the decomposition of organic material — that is, matter derived from living things. The final product, compost, is rich in essential plant nutrients and is often added to gardens. Proceeding from A to Z, this book catalogs many of the things that can be composted, such as eggshells and grass clippings, as well as some that are less obvious, such as "hair snippings" and "seaweed strands."

An obvious question that is often overlooked is: why do things rot? The simple answer is that organic material is a food source for many organisms, namely fungi, bacteria, nematodes (worms), and insects. Without the help of these small workhorses, organic material (including dead organisms) would just accumulate.

Composting is all the rage today, and for good reason. When land is farmed or when plant debris is cleared from a yard, nutrients within that plant material leave with the crops and with the yard clippings. Over time, if these nutrients are not replaced, the soil will become deficient in key elements such as iron, nitrogen, and phosphorus — as well as many others — and plants will fail to grow well. Traditionally, fertilizers have been used to replace these lost nutrients. However, fertilizers can be energy intensive to produce, and few contain all the nutrients required for plant health. Making sure to replace all the nutrients is important, because if a plant is growing in soil that is deficient in one nutrient, it will not thrive even if all the others are present. The same is true for humans; consider an individual who is deprived of a single vitamin in an otherwise well-balanced diet. The brilliance of composting, and perhaps the most important concept in this book, is that decomposed plants are a near-perfect fertilizer because they contain all the elements necessary for sustaining other plants. This is why gardeners often refer to compost as "garden gold." (Keep in mind, however, that just as with vitamins for humans, a little compost may be good for a plant, but a lot is not necessarily better.)

Digging Deeper

Talking Points

1. **Which items in the "compost stew" in the book surprised you?**
   Invite your readers to list the ingredients the children added to the compost. Which are plants? Which aren't?

2. **What would you add to your own compost stew?**
   After reading the guidelines for making your own compost stew in the "Chef's Note" at the back of the book, discuss with your readers what they might add to their own compost stew from materials in their lives. Remember, if it is not originally from a living organism, you should not put it in your compost.

3. **Why doesn't canned food rot?**
   Ask your readers why canned foods such as tomatoes, beets, beans, and peaches do not rot inside a can even though they would rot in a compost pile. Canned food has been sterilized; as a result, it is missing the requisite bacteria and fungi for breaking down organic matter. Once you open a can, no matter how carefully, bacteria and fungi have access to the contents and the food inside will begin decomposing.

Learning Experiences

1. **Observe what's happening in that compost bin.**

   Ask your readers what happens to the ingredients in compost stew. If available, add materials to an existing compost bin and track your observations. Alternatively, fill a plastic bag with some "once living" materials (e.g., cut-up fruit, grass clippings, moist bread) to make mini-decomposition chambers. Leave in the classroom or bury outside. Readers may want to experiment by providing airholes, blowing in air, or adding soil to some containers. Have them observe the containers regularly, or dig them up after a month and examine the contents.

2. **Make your own "compost stew" out of collage material.**

   Using Ashley Wolff's style for inspiration, encourage your readers to collect scraps of varied types of paper. Include newspaper, wallpaper, paint chips, cardboard, discarded photographs, and tissue paper, among others. Provide an image of a large compost bin or "stew pot" and invite your readers to tear or cut the paper into a representation of what they would put in a compost pile.

Books In Bloom: Compost Stew: An A-Z Recipe for the Earth

3. Make compost using worm bins.

Worm bins use the voracious appetite of red wigglers to decompose organic matter, whereas a compost bin relies primarily on fungi and bacteria. To start your own worm "farm," you'll need an aerated container such as a plastic bin with numerous small holes punched in the top, bedding (such as shredded newspaper), a small amount of soil, and red wigglers. Red wigglers are not the familiar earthworm, but rather a species that is particularly good at decomposing food waste — they can eat their own weight in food scraps every day — and they are easily purchased online.

Fill your worm bin three-fourths full with fluffed-up, moist — but not wet — bedding material such as shredded newspaper (1-inch strips), dead leaves, or coconut fiber (coir). This is where you'll bury food waste. Add a handful of soil to provide the grit that worms need to digest food. Keep it vegetarian, providing vegetable and fruit scraps, pulverized eggshells, coffee grounds, and tea bags. Avoid meats, dairy products, and oily foods, which can create foul odors or attract flies or rodents. Worm bins can be kept indoors or outdoors (out of the sun and heavy rains) as long as the temperature remains between 40 and 80 degrees Fahrenheit (4.4 and 26.6 Celsius).

After 2 to 3 months, most of the food and bedding will have been transformed into dark, rich compost made of worm castings, aka worm poop. If you want to keep your bin going, you will need to remove the compost and add more food. One method is to move the finished compost to one side of the bin, then place fresh bedding and food waste in the other side and let the worms migrate naturally, over time, to the fresh food and bedding. You can also dump the entire bin contents onto a plastic sheet and invite your readers to separate the worms manually. You may even see lemon-shaped cocoons, which contain between two and 20 baby worms. As your worms continue to reproduce, you will have enough to fill another bin, or to transfer to another garden.

Related Books

Water, Weed, and Wait
Written by Edith Hope Fine and
Angela Demos Halpin
Illustrated by Colleen Madden

Tricycle Press (2010)
Grade Level: K-2

· · · · · · · · ·

In the Garden with Dr. Carver (p.29)
Written by Susan Grigsby
Illustrated by Nicole Tadgell

Published by Albert Whitman
& Co. (2010)
Grade Level: 2-5

· · · · · · · · ·

Diary of a Worm
Written by Doreen Cronin
Illustrated by Harry Bliss

Published by HarperCollins (2003)
Grade Level: Pre-K-3

Decomposition Chambers

Objective	To observe and understand the process of decomposition.
Time	3 to 4 weeks
Materials	• Quart-sized plastic bags • Organic matter such as food scraps (no meat or dairy) and leaves • Inorganic matter such as marbles or Styrofoam cups • Soil • Bulletin board • Decomposition Observation Worksheet

Laying the Groundwork

Ask readers:

• **What happens to leaves in the fall?**
If leaves and other natural materials are constantly dying and falling to the ground, why are we not buried under them? (Leaves break down or decompose.)

• **What happens when people throw trash like Styrofoam or plastic cups on the ground?**
Do they disappear on their own? (Plastic takes a very long time to decompose.)

Books In Bloom: Compost Stew: An A-Z Recipe for the Earth

Exploration

1. Collect an assortment of organic and inorganic materials.
   Possible items include fruit scraps, bread, leaves, paper, marbles, and Styrofoam cups.

2. Separate the items into plastic bags.
   Fill at least two bags with the same type of material. Identify the material placed inside each bag with a label.

3. Add half a cup of moist soil to one bag of each type of material.

4. Hang your new mini-decomposition chambers on a bulletin board for observation.

5. Using the Decomposition Observation Worksheet, ask readers to predict what will happen to the items in each bag.
   Younger readers can work as a group to develop a prediction. Older readers can work in teams or on their own.

6. At least once a week for 4 weeks, give readers time to examine the bags and make notes or draw pictures about their observations.
   Do not open the bags, which may contain harmful bacteria or fungi.

7. At the end of 4 weeks, discuss findings as a group.
   Ask:
   • How did the materials in each of the bags change?
   • Which materials changed the most?
   • Did the addition of soil affect the changes? Why?

8. Generate a group list of what you learned about decomposition from this experiment.

Branching Out If time allows, test the effect of additional variables. For example, place bags in the dark or the light, store them at warm or cold temperatures, or change the moisture inside the bags.

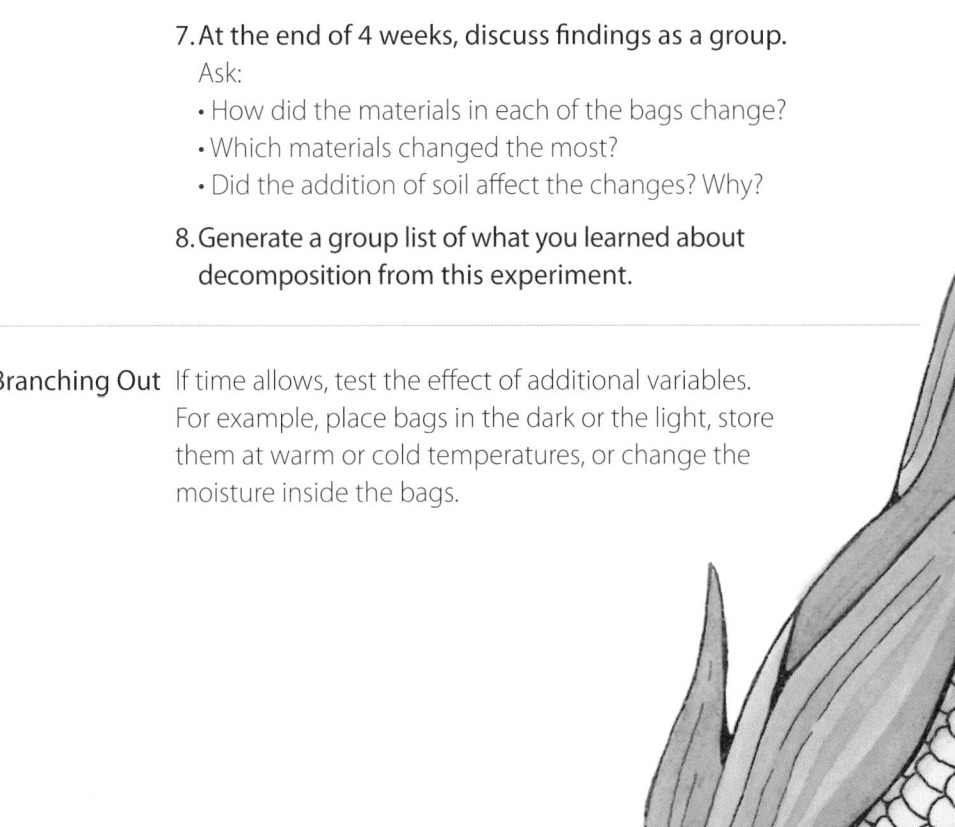

NAME   DATE

Decomposition Observation Worksheet

Sample #	Contents		What do you think will happen to the contents?	What do you observe this week?			
				Date:	Date:	Date:	Date:
		SOIL					
		NO SOIL					
		SOIL					
		NO SOIL					
		SOIL					
		NO SOIL					

Written and Illustrated by
Lane Smith

Roaring Brook Press (2011)
Grade Level: 1-4

Grandpa Green

What We Love About This Book

- Intriguing illustrations in every shade of green imaginable
- Plants as memoir

Discover the Book

Grandpa Green has garnered accolades for its illustrations, earning a Caldecott Honor and recognition as one of the New York Times 10 Best Illustrated Books of 2011. The minimalist narrative is told by a child who shares milestones of his grandfather's life as the grandfather begins to forget them. The writing offers a simple timeline, and the illustrations add depth and a sense of fantasy through topiary renditions of his life's experiences, including topiaries of such cultural icons as the Eiffel Tower. For example, the text offers the line "...but he went to a world war instead" as the illustrations capture the nature of war through abstract yet unmistakable topiary images of cannon fire, bombers, and paratroopers. A tree is cleverly converted into a cannon, complete with a wispy dandelion as the fuse, and orange leaves and flowers represent the fire spitting out of the cannon.

Readers will delight in the way that Smith uses texture and line to represent both real objects and abstract ideas. Every botanical shade of green imaginable is presented through mixed media and techniques such as pen and ink, sponge stamping, and watercolor. The story itself will be appreciated by an older audience, but all ages will enjoy identifying symbols of Grandpa's life and popular culture.

Explore the Biology

Topiary is an art form that consists of pruning plants into abstract or representative shapes such as obelisks or chickens. Created by the Romans, topiary gardens have historically been a sign of wealth. The range of possible shapes that can be formed is large, determined by patience, skill, and imagination; the number of plants that can be shaped, however, is quite small. Plants that do well as topiary, such as boxwood, privet, and holly, are able to withstand heavy pruning and typically have the dense foliage required for shaping.

From the biological perspective, what we like about this book is that it explores the relationship between gardening and art. Many gardens embody artistic elements such as color and composition, but in this story, the plants are transformed into representational art such as characters from The Wizard of Oz or a wedding cake. Topiary has the capacity to delight because the transformation of the plant is so unexpected. For example, a bush shaped into a dragon is both surprising and intriguing.

Digging Deeper

Talking Points

1. **Which images are realistic and which are fantastical?**
   Topiary is a real art form, yet the picture-book format allows Lane Smith to use a mix of both realistic and imaginary topiary. Ask your reader which topiary sculptures made them smile? Which could actually be created out of plants and which use artistic license?

2. **Why does Grandpa Green make shapes out of plants?**
   How did he choose which shapes to make? Invite your reader to notice the shapes represented by the plants. Some are personal milestones (his birthday cake, his first kiss, his chicken pox), and others are more general, such as an elephant or the Eiffel Tower. Open the gatefold page at the end of the book and ask your readers to identify the topiary figures. Have your readers make a pictorial timeline to represent their understanding of the milestones in Grandpa Green's life.

3. **How exactly does Lane Smith use plants to convey details?**
   The limited color and use of plant images in the award-winning illustrations is what makes them so visually intriguing. For example, on the page where we read "in fourth grade, he got chicken pox (not from chickens)," through plants, we can tell that he has chicken pox, he's in bed, and his hair is unkempt. Smith conveys this all with a palette of hedges, berries, twigs, and leaves. With your readers, examine the war cannon page and ask them to describe what is happening and how it is represented by the artist.

Books In Bloom: Grandpa Green

Learning Experiences

1. Make a topiary.

Sculpting plants into topiary is a long process that can take years, but for more immediate success, you can sculpt or paint with moss. Moss grows easily on a brick or stone surface, allowing you to create a moss-covered sculpture. Gather a handful of moss and place it in a blender with 2 cups of buttermilk, 2 cups of water, and 1 teaspoon of sugar. Puree the mixture and pour it into a spray bottle or use a paintbrush to disperse it. You can paint a two-dimensional picture with moss on a wall or sidewalk, or you can build a three-dimensional sculpture using stones or bricks. Be sure that your creation is in the shade and that you mist it regularly to promote moss growth. To encourage connections with Grandpa Green, challenge readers to create moss sculptures or pictures that represent their own life experiences. "Rough drafts" can be made with sponge painting.

2. Create art using unexpected materials.

Topiary is engaging because a plant is transformed into a recognizable shape. The author has fun with this idea and assembles plant parts together that would never occur in nature. Where else have you seen unexpected art? An example might be a clock made from an old bicycle gear chain. Choose an important event or figure in your life and create some unexpected art from recycled objects.

3. Sponge-paint your life.

Have your readers select an important event in their lives. It could be a personal memory or a story they have been told about a birthday party, trip, moving, or other significant event. Have readers describe this experience using only one or two brief sentences and then draft an illustration. Add color by sponge painting to create a look similar to the topiaries in the book. Green is an essential color for this activity. Make different shades of green by mixing small amounts of yellow, blue, red, white, and black. It may be fun to collect green paint samples from the local hardware store for inspiration.

Related Books

Moss Art

Objective	To create living artwork.

Time	4 weeks

Materials
- Brick or stone surface or statue
- Moss
- 2 cups buttermilk
- 2 cups water
- 1 teaspoon sugar
- Blender
- Paintbrush

Laying the Groundwork

Ask readers:

- **What is topiary?**
  What do you think are some of the challenges in creating topiaries? (Topiaries are sculptures created through a process of pruning plants to create three-dimensional shapes. Careful pruning is necessary to maintain plant health. It can take many years to train plants into topiaries.)

- **What is moss?**
  (Mosses are simple plants.)

- **In what ways is living artwork different from traditional paintings and sculptures?**
  (It is intended to change over time.)

Exploration

1. **Find a base for your artwork.**

   A surface that is somewhat porous like brick or stone is preferable because it allows the moss rhizoids (rootlike structures of moss plants) to take hold. You can choose a flat surface and make a two-dimensional graffiti-like design, or find a statue to create a three-dimensional effect. Moss needs sunlight for photosynthesis, but too much sun will cause it to dry out quickly, so a location in partial shade is best. Keep in mind that your moss creation does not need to be permanent. Most moss sculptures can be removed with a strong spray of water; if that does not work, you can spray it with lime juice and the acid will take care of any remaining plant materials.

2. **Gather moss.**

   Moss can often be found in shady, damp locations like wooded areas or along streams. One or two handfuls will probably be enough for a single design.

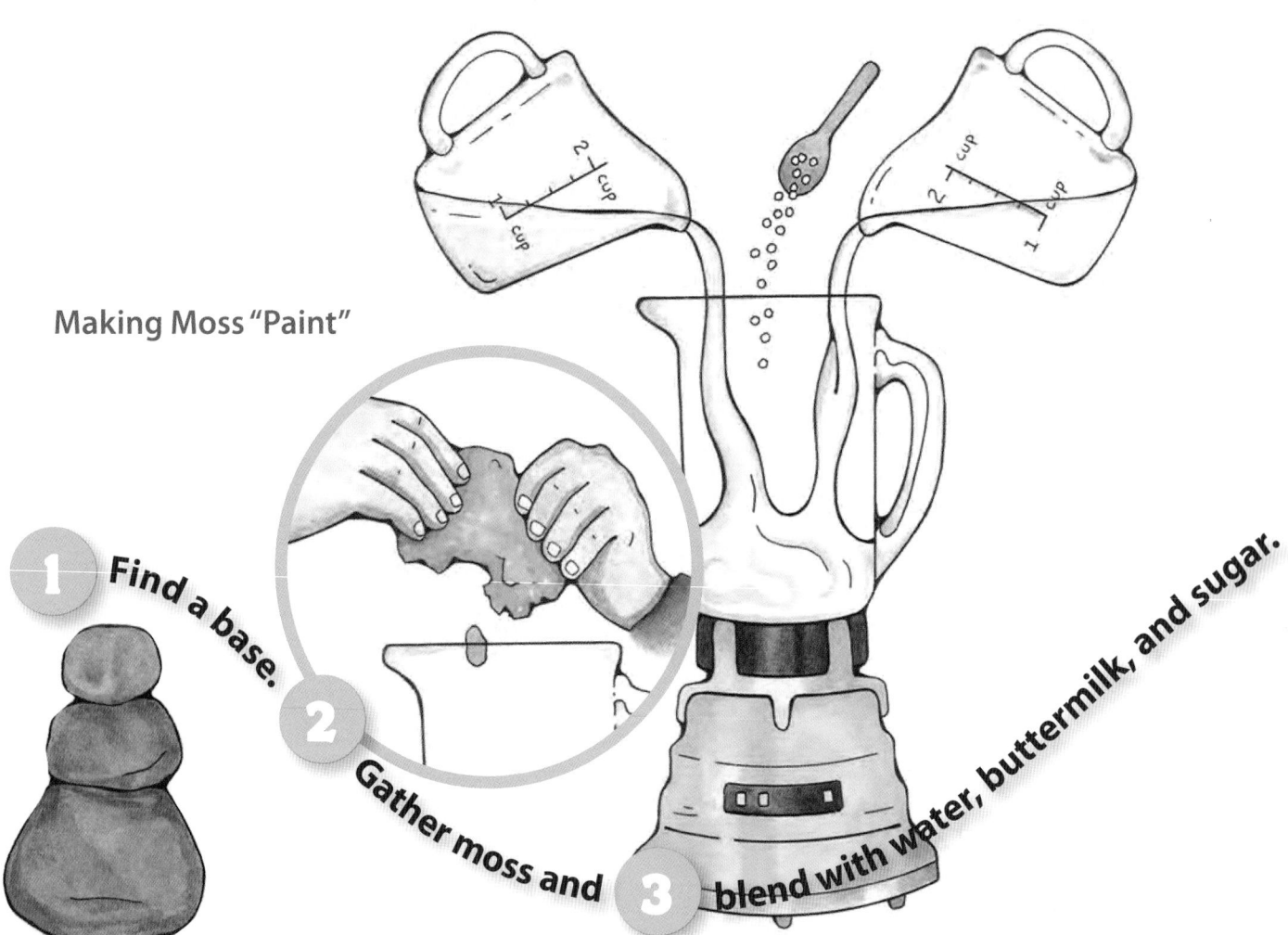

Making Moss "Paint"

1 Find a base.

2 Gather moss and

3 blend with water, buttermilk, and sugar.

3. Place the moss, along with 2 cups of buttermilk, 2 cups of water, and 1 teaspoon of sugar, into a blender.
   Puree the mixture. The desired consistency is similar to paint.

4. Apply the moss mixture with a paintbrush, or disperse it using a spray bottle (be aware that it can easily clog the sprayer).
   If creating a wall display, use chalk to draw an outline first.

5. Carefully monitor moisture for the first few weeks to allow the moss to take hold.
   Mist gently and regularly.

Branching Out   Research examples of topiary gardens. Ladew Topiary Garden in Maryland is a great place to start (*www.ladewgardens.com/HOME.aspx*). Have readers create designs for their own topiary garden. Use sponge art to mimic the illustrations in Grandpa Green.

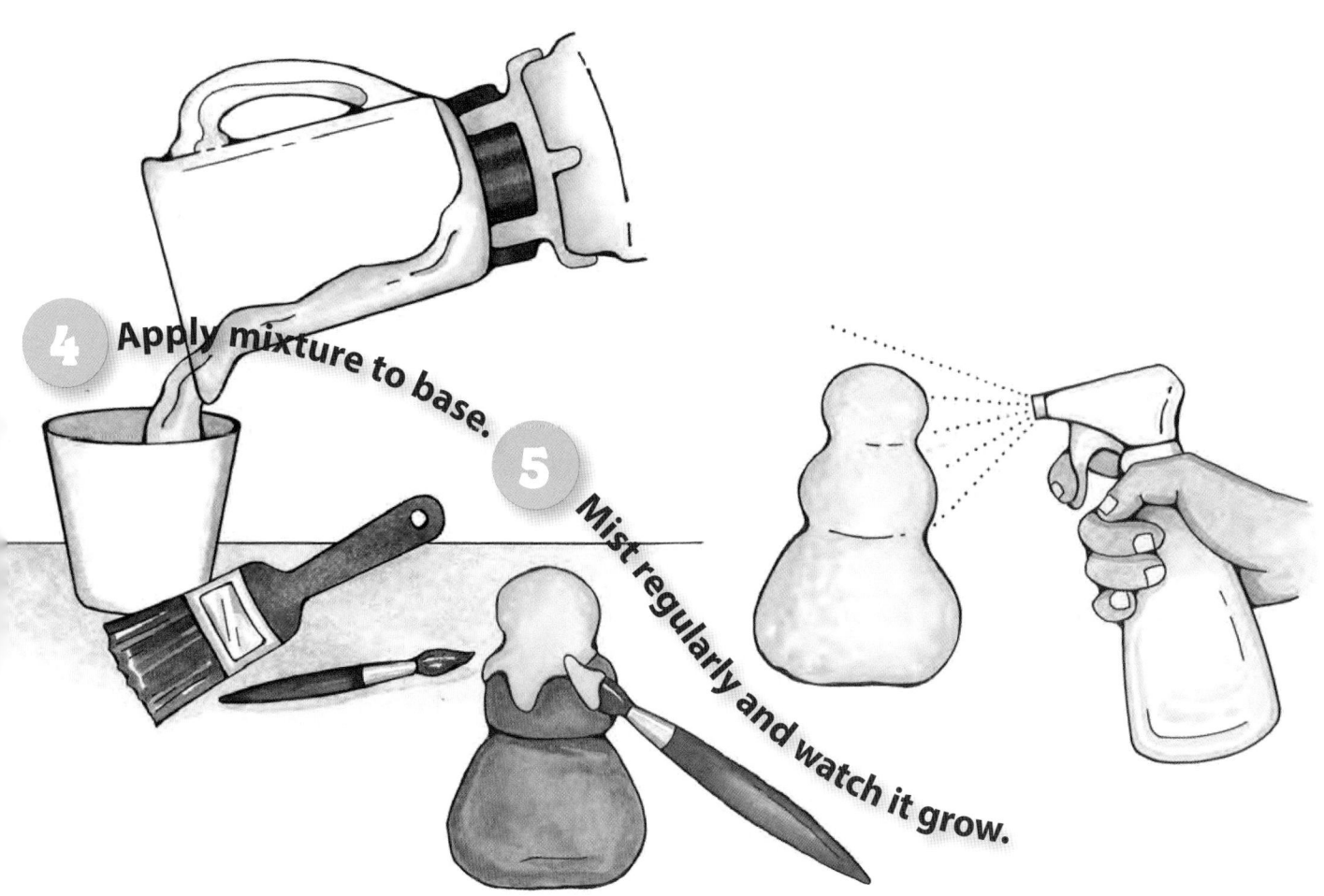

4 Apply mixture to base.

5 Mist regularly and watch it grow.

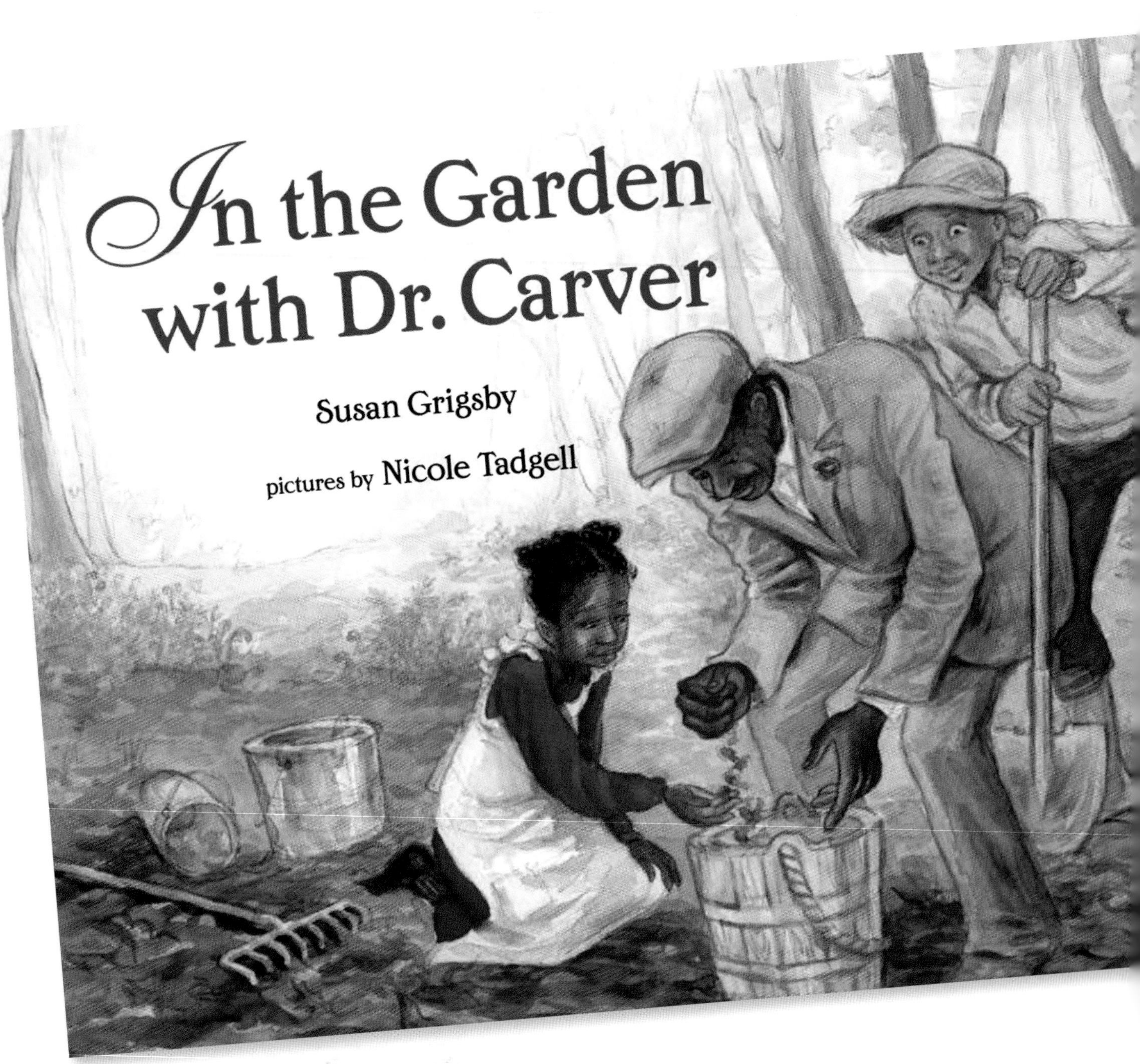

In the Garden with Dr. Carver

Susan Grigsby

pictures by Nicole Tadgell

Written by Susan Grigsby
Illustrated by Nicole Tadgell

• • • • • • •

Published by Albert Whitman
& Co. (2010)
Grade Level: 2-5

In the Garden with Dr. Carver

What We Love About This Book

- Bringing a historical icon to life
- The connection drawn between the scientific method and farming
- "Chicken" made out of peanuts

Discover the Book

Proponents of the movement to eat locally grown foods owe a nod of thanks to Dr. George Washington Carver, a famous post–Civil War agricultural innovator who set out to help farmers grow their own food and diversify their crops. This work of historical fiction offers a glimpse of the factual Dr. Carver and how he used his traveling educational wagon to help establish teaching and school gardens throughout Alabama in the early 1900s. Told through the eyes of an enthusiastic schoolgirl named Sally, the story offers as much agricultural information in its 32 pages as Dr. Carver packed into a carefully planned garden. Dr. Carver spends a day at Sally's school, where the class learns how to prepare soil, make observations about growing conditions, create compost, and cook from the garden. Sally and Dr. Carver are the main characters, but we also see the change and growth in the garden itself as the story progresses. Important biological concepts such as life cycles, ecosystems, and competition are addressed simply but accurately through conversations between Dr. Carver and the children. For example, the students learn to pick dandelion weeds so that they don't compete for food, light, and water with the flowers their teacher has planted.

Watercolor illustrations support many of the ideas detailed in the text, such as the comparison of the growing conditions of two rosebushes or the words Jesup Agricultural Wagon painted in honor of the benefactor of this "movable school." The facial expressions of the characters humorously convey both nuances and overt elements of the story, such as the surprise of tasting "chicken" made of peanuts. Perhaps the most satisfying illustration is tucked away on the copyright page (found at the end) of Sally matching the size of a cabbage to a friend's head, as promised in Dr. Carver's initial pitch about the benefits of his gardening techniques. Readers who love details will enjoy the field-guide style of the end pages, where specific flora and fauna related to the school garden are shown individually with common and Latin names.

Explore the Biology

During Reconstruction, many African-Americans found themselves living as subsistence farmers on land that was nutrient-stripped from decades of cotton monocropping. The cotton harvest of the South was further plagued by the appearance of a new pest, the cotton boll weevil. This top-notch book tells the story of how Dr. George Washington Carver changed the farming culture in the Southern African-American communities from cotton monocropping to diversified farms with higher yields that provided food security. Dr. Carver believed "a well kept garden should furnish directly and indirectly one-half of the food supply of the family, besides going a long way toward keeping the family healthy" (Help for The Hard Times, Carver). Dr. Carver reached his audience through short farming manuals and a traveling school run out of his wagon. His message — shared by the modern organic gardening movement — advocated soil health, diversity, beneficial organisms, and value-added crops.

In the text, Dr. Carver offers the simple yet important advice to be an observant grower. Observation allows farmers and gardeners to recognize trends and make informed decisions. This message is emphasized when Dr. Carver asks Sally to compare two rosebushes, one that is thriving and another that is struggling. Sally correctly observes that the two differ only in available light, conveying the "right plant–right place" principle of growing.

Nutrients Cycle: From Soil to Plant and back again.

Soil is the unsung hero of the gardening world; plants get their nutrients from this medium. Although plants use light as an energy source and to make sugars out of CO_2 through photosynthesis, plants also, just like people, need nutrients or vitamins to grow. This is where soil comes in. Imagine a person on a diet of sugar and water, similar to a plant getting only light and water — both would have energy available, but would also need vitamins and nutrients to metabolize it. Plants may get their energy through photosynthesis, but they obtain necessary nutrients from the soil. This concept is conveyed directly and indirectly through the teachings of Dr. Carver, who advocates growing plants that enrich the soil, such as peanuts (a nitrogen-fixing legume), and amending the soil with "leaf mulch" and "swamp muck."

Books In Bloom: In the Garden with Dr. Carver

Nutrient cycling and ecosystems are also prevalent in this book. Dr. Carver tells Sally's brother, "That spider is helping your garden by eating up the creatures that want to eat your plants. Before you change or destroy something, you need to understand why it exists and its relationship with the rest of nature. The plants, the soil, and the animals that visit are all connected, just like a web." That one passage captures the idea that the well-being of one species is often dependent upon that of another. Just as a plant's life cycle can be described as proceeding from seed to seed, the cycle of nutrients goes from soil to soil by passing through an organism and then back to soil as decaying organic matter.

Digging Deeper

Talking Points

1. How did Dr. Carver make a difference?

   Dr. Carver is recognized as one of the greatest figures of his time. In 1949, Life magazine called him a modern-day Leonardo da Vinci for his inventions. Ask your readers, "*What can we glean from the book about how Dr. Carver made a difference? For example, how might Sally and her brother's lives be different because of Dr. Carver?*"

2. How did Dr. Carver direct the students to prepare the soil?

   All gardeners and farmers start by preparing the soil. Ask your readers what they would do if they were going to start a garden. Ask how Dr. Carver and the children prepared the soil to get it ready for their garden. Answers may include: clearing stones, rocks, and debris, adding compost, and "turning and mixing."

3. Why is amending the soil important to plant health?

   In the book, Dr. Carver uses comparisons with the human body to help the children understand that plants need nutrients from the soil in order to survive. Ask your readers to list nutritious food for people. Many foods on this list will be plants. Where did the plants get these nutrients? Guide your readers to notice the importance of rich soil in plant health as shown in the book. If your list of nutritious foods includes animals or animal products, lead your readers to the realization that the animals got their nutrients from plants as well.

Learning Experiences

1. Explore soil and determine its composition.

Soil is made up of sand, silt, and clay particles derived from rock broken down over thousands of years by climatic and environmental conditions (rain, glaciers, wind, rivers, animals, and other natural forces). Sand particles are the largest and feel gritty in your fingers. Silt particles are medium-sized and feel similar to flour. Clay particles are the smallest, and can be seen only with a microscope. In addition to sand, silt, and clay, soil contains organic matter (decaying plant and animal material) and pore space that allows water and air to move through the soil.

The proportions of each type of particle determine the soil characteristics. For example, soil with a high proportion of sand drains quickly; soil high in clay tends to be compact and retain water. Soils that have roughly equal amounts of sand, silt, and clay are called loam.

To determine your soil composition, fill a clear container two-thirds full of water, then add a sample of soil until it almost reaches the top. Shake vigorously and set aside for 1 to 2 days until the soil particles settle to the bottom. The particles will settle in three layers: sand, silt, and clay, with sand at the bottom, and organic matter will float to the top. The thickness of each layer is the proportion of that type of particle in the soil. Ask your readers to figure out the most common particle in the soil and then describe the composition using words such as sandy, silty, mostly clay, or loam. Challenge them to estimate the percentage of particle type by measuring the height of each layer and then dividing by the total height of the soil in the container.

2. Demonstrate how healthy soil results in happy plants.

To reinforce the importance of healthy soil, try growing two sets of plants in different types of soils. Fill an even number of cups with sand — a nutrient-poor medium — and to half of them add organic matter such as compost or even decaying leaves. Plant quick-growing seeds, such as radishes, in both; place the cups in a well-lit window; and water them regularly. Observe what happens over the following weeks. You may find it revealing to measure number of leaves produced, plant height, coloration, and plant weight.

3. Create a garden calendar.

Although the book captures just a single day in the garden, Dr. Carver's historical pamphlets outline monthly tasks for creating and maintaining a garden. Working with your readers, create a gardening calendar for your area. Some possible elements to include: soil preparation, planting dates determined primarily by average daily temperature or frost potential, and harvest time. Compare your calendar to the dates used by farmers and gardeners in your area by searching online for "planting schedule" and the name of your state.

Additional Resource

Dr. Carver's first pamphlet offering the basics for a self-sufficient farm may be seen at this link: *http://inventors.about.com/od/stepbystep/ss/Hard_Times.htm*

Related Books

First Garden: The White House Garden
Written and Illustrated by Robbin Gourley

Published by Clarion Books (2011)
Grade Level: 1-4

. . . .

Water, Weed, and Wait
Written by Edith Hope Fine and Angela Demos Halpin
Illustrated by Colleen Madden

Published by Tricycle Press (2010)
Grade Level: K-2

. . . .

Compost Stew: An A to Z Recipe for the Earth (p.14)
Written by Mary McKenna Siddals
Illustrated by Ashley Wolff

Published by Tricycle Press (2010)
Grade Level: K-4

Soil Sleuths

Objective	To compare ways to determine soil composition.
Time	2 days
Materials	• Soil sample • Water • A clear jar or plastic bottle • Ruler • Soil composition worksheet

Laying the Groundwork

Ask readers:

• **Why is soil important to plant health?**
(Plants need nutrients from the soil in order to survive.)

• **What is soil made of?**
(Soil is made up of sand, silt, and clay particles derived from rock broken down over thousands of years by climatic and environmental conditions [rain, glaciers, wind, rivers, animals, and other natural forces]. Sand particles are the largest and feel gritty in your fingers. Silt particles are medium-sized and feel similar to flour. Clay particles are the smallest, and can be seen only with a microscope. In addition to sand, silt, and clay, soil contains organic matter [decaying plant and animal material] and pore space that allows water and air to move through the soil.)

Make a "Mudshake"

Fill a jar with water and soil!

Shake, shake, shake, shake.

See where everything has settled overnight.

Organic Material
Water
Clay
Silt
Gravel and Sand

Exploration

1. Explain to readers that they will explore soil composition using two different techniques.

2. Conduct the "Ribbon Test":
   Take a small clump of soil and add water until it makes a moist ball. Next, rub the soil together between your fingers. If the soil makes a nice, long ribbon, then it has a lot of clay in it (thus sticks together well). If it crumbles in your hand, then it has a lot of sand. If it is somewhere in between, then you probably have a good mix. Record results on the soil composition worksheet.

3. Conduct the "Shake It Up Test":
   Make "mudshakes" and then watch the different components settle out. (a) Fill a clear container about two-thirds full of water, then add enough soil to nearly fill the jar. (b) Shake the jar vigorously, then (c) let it sit overnight to allow the particles to settle into layers. The larger particles (gravel and sand) are heaviest and will settle at the bottom, followed by silt; the last full layer will be clay. The clay may stay suspended and cloud the water for a long time. Organic matter will float on or just below the water surface. Using a ruler, first measure each layer, and then determine the approximate percentage of each component. Record on the soil composition worksheet.

4. Compare the results of the "Shake It Up Test" to those of the "Ribbon Test."
   What are the benefits and drawbacks of each method? Which test is more accurate?

Branching Out Purchase a soil testing kit at a local garden center to find out the nutrient content of your soil. Most kits will provide an indicator for the amount of nitrogen, phosphorus, and potassium present in a sample. These are the three nutrients plants use in the largest quantities.

If time and money allow, you can also send a soil sample to your state's soil laboratory for more precise results and compare them with the tests you completed on your own.

Books In Bloom: In the Garden with Dr. Carver

NAME _____   DATE _____

Soil Composition Worksheet

Ribbon Test

Our soil is mostly made up of (circle one):

Sand	Clay	Loam
(the ribbon is crumbly)	(it makes a long, sticky ribbon)	(it's a good mixture of sand, silt, and clay)

Shake It Up Test

Soil Layer Heights

Sand (bottom layer) Height: _____   Clay (top layer) Height: _____

Silt (middle layer) Height: _____   Height of all layers: _____

Soil Component Percentages

Percentage of Sand: _____
(height of sand layer/height of all layers x 100)

Percentage of Silt: _____
(height of silt layer/height of all layers x 100)

Percentage of Clay: _____
(height of clay layer/height of all layers x 100)

Visual Breakdown

Draw the layers of soil in your jar.

Written and Illustrated by
Henry Cole

· · · · · · · ·

Greenwillow Books (1995)
Grade Level: K-3

Jack's Garden

What We Love About This Book

- Cumulative text
- So many types of ladybugs

Discover the Book

This story is about a boy named Jack who plants a garden in the spring. The book follows the development of his garden over the growing season using cumulative text and informative illustrations. Borrowing from the pattern of the classic tale "The House That Jack Built," the author adds a new line on each page, incorporating gardening vocabulary to describe the sequence of the growing garden. This style lends itself to reading aloud and offers reading support through the use of repetition and predictability. The length and complexity of the text parallels the growth of the garden. In the spring, the garden is described in a single sentence, "This is the garden that Jack planted"; over the summer, the garden grows, and the text lengthens.

Detailed colored pencil illustrations enhance the simple text in two distinct ways. Each page features a framed box; within it, Jack's garden forms pictorially over the course of one growing season. Bordering this box are illustrations that provide the opportunity to delve more deeply into certain aspects of the natural world, such as insects, plant development, cloud formation, and floral diversity.

Explore the Biology

This is truly a gardener's book, with illustrations and text that accurately represent the key biological and gardening events of a growing season. The story can be used to explore the fundamental elements of plant growth, gardening, and the plant life cycle. Readers learn what is required to start a garden, and learn that plants need soil, water, and light to grow. On the merit of this alone, Jack's Garden is useful; however, what we love about this book is that it provides a glimpse into the complexity of nature. This idea is developed through the border illustrations. For example, on one are drawings of different types of ladybugs; readers may be surprised to learn that ladybug is a generic term and in actuality there are many different types. The presentation of both the generic and the specific helps convey that the natural world is both diverse and complex.

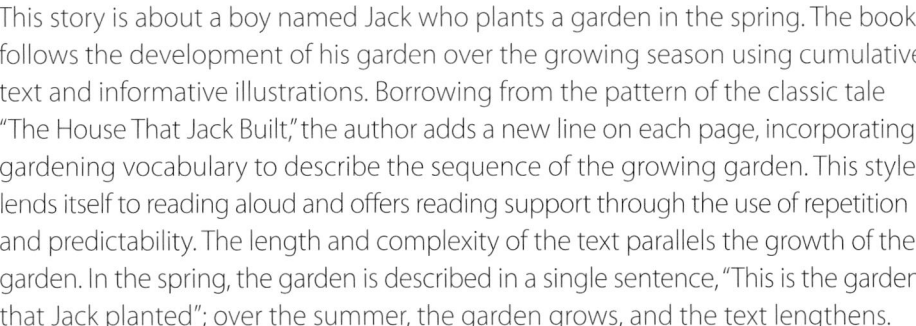

 **Digging Deeper**

Talking Points

1. What's the pattern?

Ask readers what they notice about the way the text is written. Help them recognize the pattern, in which each page adds a new line of text and a new detail about gardening in a cumulative and rhythmic way.

2. How do people work with nature to create gardens?

A garden is planted by people, but greatly affected by nature. Begin your discussion by having your readers look through the book to identify the natural elements and their respective roles in the garden. For example, seeds, rain, and pollinators are all contributors to the garden. After your readers have identified the "cast," ask them to explain the role of Jack, the rain, the seeds, or any of the other "characters" in the garden. If you removed one of these elements, would the garden still succeed, and if so, how?

3. What are the steps required to make a garden?

Use the book to create a classroom gardening guide to share with others. Steps will include: prepare the soil, plant seeds, water seeds; seeds will sprout, plants will grow, plants will bloom; insects will pollinate the flowers; seeds will develop so the cycle can begin again.

Learning Experiences

1. Use generic and specific words.

Why do words matter? Gardeners benefit from using terminology to distinguish organisms in the same category from one another. For example, the category "plant" does not tell you as much as rose or pumpkin. Similarly, for people, we use individual names rather than categorical terms such as child or adult. Ask your readers what it would be like to spend a day with their friends without using their names. They will quickly grasp the difficulty of communicating using general terms. The same is true in the garden.

2. Lead a choral reading.

This book lends itself to repeated readings. Invite listeners to take turns being responsible for each phrase, with all chiming in on "the garden that Jack planted." Younger readers might enjoy creating movements to go with their lines.

3. Make your own desktop garden.

Have your readers plant a desktop flower garden in a clear plastic cup with fast growing seeds such as zinnias or marigolds. Paralleling Jack's Garden, have your readers illustrate their own sequential book. For example, on the first page, the book reads, "This is the garden that Jack planted," and the illustrations show the garden tools Jack used. In their own books, have your readers draw the materials they used to assemble their desktop garden. Have them continue to parallel the book as their gardens grow, adding new entries as appropriate. The title, of course, will be individualized, as in Nell's Garden or Zander's Garden.

Related Books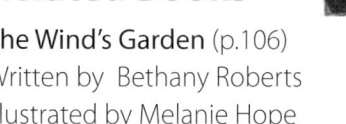

The Wind's Garden (p.106)
Written by Bethany Roberts
Illustrated by Melanie Hope Greenberg

Henry Holt (2001)
Grade Level: K-2

· · · · · · ·

The House I'll Build for the Wrens
Written by Shirley Neitzel
Illustrated by Nancy Winslow Parker

Published by Greenwillow Books (1997)
Grade Level: K-2

The Importance of Words

Objective   To demonstrate the value of using specific words instead of general words.

Time   1 hour

Materials
• Journals
• Pencils

Laying the Groundwork   Ask your readers to close their eyes as you read the following two statements:
"The garden is filled with beautiful plants"
and
"The garden is filled with beautiful roses, sunflowers, and tomatoes."

Ask readers:

• **What does each sentence tell you, and when would you use one versus the other?**
(The second sentence provides detailed information. You would use the second sentence when describing the garden to someone who could not see it.)

• **Why do words matter?**
(Using specific words instead of general words helps us communicate information clearly because the listener or reader can visualize what is being said.)

Exploration

1. **Take your readers to a lawn or green space and ask them what they see.**

   They will probably give a general description such as grass, trees, and lawn. Next, ask them to identify two different plants and use specific terms to distinguish between them. For example, you might find different grasses, clover, and, if you are lucky, a dandelion, all of which are plants, but have distinguishing features. Other generic possibilities include rocks and clouds. How might someone describe one cloud so specifically that others could identify it?

2. **Explain to your readers that specific details are often overlooked but contribute to the overall picture of this green space.**

   See if you can identify the role of each of the things you observe. For example, what is the role of earthworms? (One possible response: they burrow through the soil and create air space so plant roots can grow.)

3. **Next, if you have an outdoor garden, take your readers there; if not, go to another natural area.**

   Have readers identify something they see in this location that interests them (e.g., cardinal, sunflower, large rock, or other object).

4. **Have your readers write a description of this object in their journals.**

   They should start the descriptions with more general terms and then use more specific details as they progress. Be sure that the descriptions don't use the actual name of the object, but only describe it.

5. **Have your readers read their lists to a partner, one descriptive word or phrase at a time.**

   The partner will try to guess what the object is, given the descriptive words. If the object isn't guessed with the first word, the partner should give the next descriptive word or phrase on the list until either the partner guesses correctly, or the name of the object is shared. The idea is to figure out what the object is with as few clues as possible. For example:
   - Descriptive words ranging from general to specific: small, living, wings, animal, two legs, bird, blue
   - Answer: blue jay

6. **Conclude by brainstorming all the benefits of using specific words.**

Branching Out Observe characteristics of similar things in the garden. Group readers and assign each of them a category of organism typically found in gardens, such as birds, insects, or plants. Groups should generate a list to distinguish between the different species within their category. For example, the bird group could distinguish differences between cardinals, blue jays, and crows, while the insect group could identify differences between praying mantises, ants, crickets, and other insects. Once students have made their own distinctions, use field guides for each category to learn how these species are typically distinguished, using features such as marks, colors, sizes, shapes, and behaviors.

Have the groups create their own field guide for the categories they observed in the garden. These could serve as an educational piece to display in the garden or could be included in a garden brochure or newsletter.

Books In Bloom: Jack's Garden

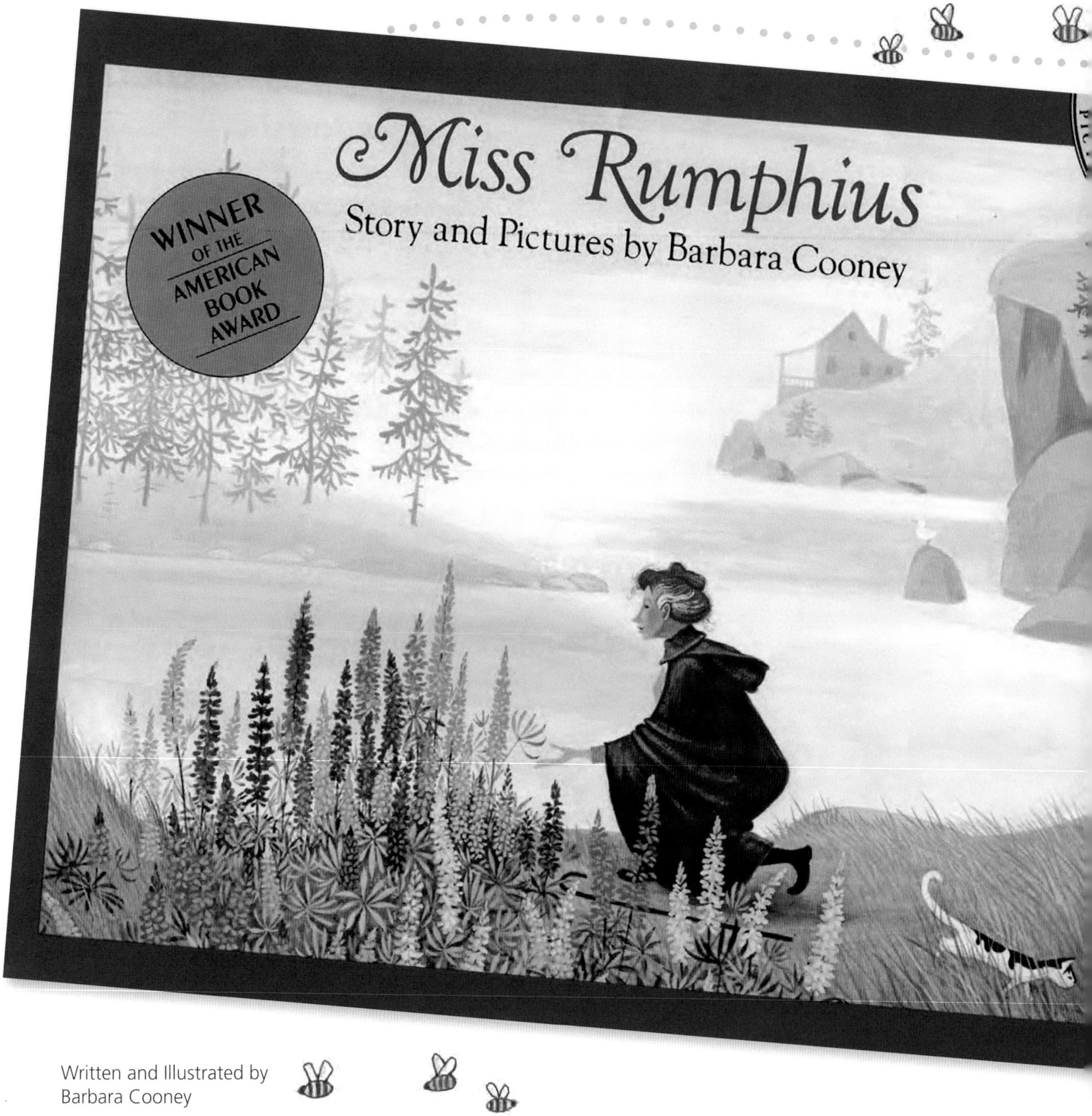

Miss Rumphius
Story and Pictures by Barbara Cooney

WINNER OF THE AMERICAN BOOK AWARD

Written and Illustrated by
Barbara Cooney

Published by Viking (1982)
Grade Level: K-2

43

Miss Rumphius

What We Love About This Book

- The essence of Maine conveyed in illustrations
- Celebrating the lupine

Discover the Book

Little Alice Rumphius admires her grandfather's well-traveled past and vows that she too will see faraway places and eventually live beside the sea. Her grandfather, who carves figureheads for ships, challenges her to do a third thing: find a way to make the world more beautiful. Once she is grown, Alice works in a library, and reads about faraway places. She travels solo around the world during the Victorian era, living fully and learning all she can. Long after her travels, she settles in a seaside cottage. One day, she falls seriously ill. When the cool pink, lavender, and blue of lupine flowers bring cheer to her bedside window, she is inspired to spread their colors throughout her coastal community. In a circular plot ending, Miss Rumphius's great-niece, Alice, ponders how to make the world more beautiful.

The delicate acrylic illustrations capture Maine's craggy coastline, and the lupines' pointy leaves and towering blossoms are clearly recognizable. Readers will pick up details of period architecture, artwork, and a comfortable life. The dual messages of living life fully and contributing to the broader world will be readily understood by children of all ages. Cooney's powerful story and pleasing illustrations earned her an American Booksellers' Association National Book Award in 1983 and have inspired several "Miss Rumphius" teaching awards for educators who make a difference.

Explore the Biology

At first pass this book may seem to be about seed dispersal, but upon closer examination we see it is really about the act of sowing seeds or planting. True seed dispersal relies on co-opted agents such as wind, water, or animals, for which the act of moving the seed is not deliberate. Sowing and planting, on the other hand, are intentional acts. In nature, lupine seeds are dispersed by the dried seed pod, which, with the wind, acts as a catapult to spread the seeds away from the parent plant. In this story, Miss Rumphius disperses lupine seeds in locations that she feels need beautification.

This act is very similar to the emerging movement called guerrilla gardening, which originated in the United Kingdom. Guerrilla gardeners strive to make the world a more beautiful place by transforming urban blight with "seed bombs" or secret plantings. Just as Miss Rumphius sowed seeds to beautify her area of coastal Maine, these activists may use disguises and the cover of night to sow seeds in places like abandoned lots, unkempt roadsides, and potholes.

 **Digging Deeper**

Talking Points

1. **What do the illustrations tell us about Alice's life as a child?**

   Ask your readers to look, for example, at the picture of Alice wearing a blue dress and sitting on her grandfather's lap, or the one where she is helping him in his workshop. Have readers describe what is happening in these pictures and compare these activities to their own lives.

2. **How might your readers make the world a more beautiful place?**

   Have them list some ideas that involve plants. Miss Rumphius's idea was fairly simple, but it worked. Ask your readers how she did it and what they would need to implement their ideas.

3. **Why do people sow seeds?**

   Why did Miss Rumphius sow seeds, as opposed to just letting nature run its course? What is gained (and lost) by sowing versus relying on nature? Discussion topics here might include growing crops for food, which would require sowing, and maximizing use of space.

Learning Experiences

1. **Be a guerrilla gardener.**

   Find a safe local area to beautify through guerrilla gardening, and make sure you are permitted to do so. Make seeds bombs with your readers, as shown in the illustrations in the Lesson Plan below, and disperse them in your chosen spot.

2. **Discover the importance of "right plant, right place."**

   Miss Rumphius was able to beautify her environment with minimal effort because lupines grow naturally in meadows, and their seeds can be sown directly onto the ground. Not just any type of seed would grow this easily. Plants that can thrive without our help are said to have "weedy" characteristics. For example, you may see chicory, dandelions, and raspberries growing on their own, but rarely see "volunteer" corn or delphiniums. With your readers, collect seeds from self-sown plants (such as native plants or weeds) and also collect seeds from plants grown by humans. Sow them as Miss Rumphius did, emulating her technique of avoiding soil preparation and maintenance. Predict which plants will survive and why. Keep track of the results, bearing in mind that success will be influenced by germination as well as the ability to grow and compete in that environment.

3. **Learn about key flowers in your area.**

   Ask your readers to list the flowers, trees, or plants that are associated with their geographic area. Explore why these plants are iconic in your region by asking your readers about their cultural, biological, or historical significance. Create a guide to help identify these important plants.

Related Books

The Wind's Garden (p.106)
Written by Bethany Roberts
Illustrated by Melanie Hope Greenberg

Published by Henry Holt (2001)
Grade Level: K-2

• • • • • • • •

Planting the Wild Garden
Written by Kathryn O. Galbraith
Illustrated by Wendy Anderson Halperin

Published by Peachtree Publishers (2011)
Grade Level: K-2

• • • • • • • •

A Fruit Is a Suitcase for Seeds (p.1)
Written by Jean Richards
Illustrated by Anca Hariton

Published by The Millbrook Press (2002)
Grade Level: K-2

• • • • • • • •

The Plant Hunters: True Stories of Their Daring Adventures to the Far Corners of the Earth
Written by Anita Silvey
Illustrators: (Compilation)

Published by Farrar, Straus and Giroux (2012)
Grade Level: 2-5

 **Lesson Plan**

Seed Bombs

Objective	To make seed bombs to be used for easy planting in cultivated or uncultivated areas.
Time	1 hour
Materials	• Clay (available from craft stores) • Compost or potting soil • Seeds (easy-to-grow or native varieties)

Laying the Groundwork	Ask readers:
	• Where would you throw your seed bombs and why?
	  (Suggest areas around the school or community.)
	
	• What might happen if we just spread seeds on the ground?
	  (They might wash away with rain or blow away with wind, or be eaten by birds or other animals.)

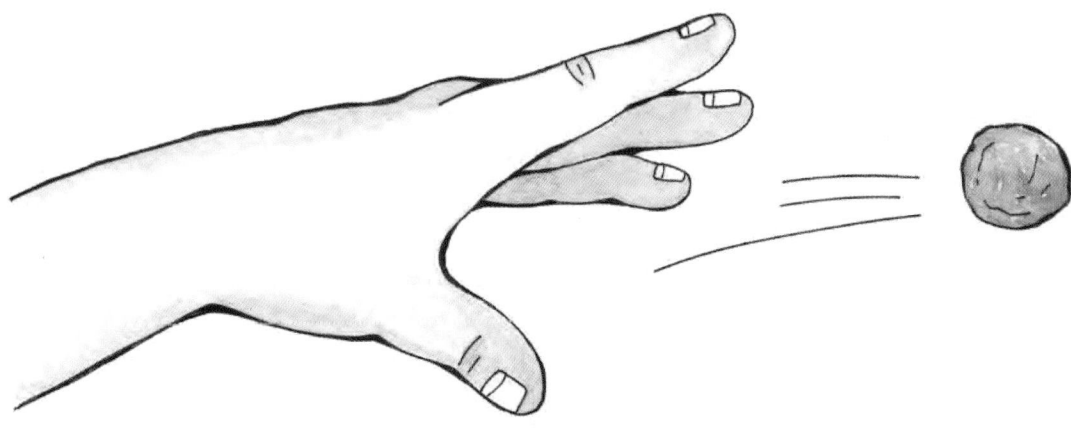

Exploration

1. **Explain to readers that you are going to create "seed bombs,"** small balls that combine seeds, compost or potting soil (which provide some nutrients), and clay (which helps keep the seeds in the same place until they can sprout and take root). Seed bombing dates back to the 1930s, when compressed bundles of soil containing live plants were dropped out of airplanes to help re-vegetate areas. It is still used today to help replant large areas burned by wildfires.

2. **Take a walk through your neighborhood or schoolyard.** Is there a vacant lot or an abandoned space? Make that small patch of land into something beautiful for everyone to see by dropping a seed bomb!

3. **Divide your materials so you have:**
   - 5 parts clay
   - 1 part compost/potting soil
   - 1 part seeds

4. **Combine the clay and compost.** Add a little water if your mixture is dry. The mixture should be moist but not dripping wet.

5. **Add the seeds to the clay and compost.** Thoroughly work the materials together with your hands.

6. **Shape the mixture into a ball.** Your bomb should be about the size of a golf ball.

7. **Plant or air dry: you can either plant your seed bomb while it is still moist or allow it to dry.** As long as it is watered (either manually or by rain) once it's planted, the clay will break down and the seeds will grow.

8. **Keep an eye on the area and enjoy the beauty!** Ask readers to maintain a journal about the plants' progress and the impact of the flowering plants on the site and community.

Branching Out Create experiments to investigate which methods for creating seed bombs result in the greatest success in plant establishment. Try using different types of seeds, different sizes of clay balls, and different locations. Track seed germination and number of plants that survive until maturity.

by Helen Frost
Illustrated by Leonid Gore

*Published by Atheneum Books
for Young Readers (2008)
Grade Level: K-3*

Books In Bloom: Monarchs and Milkweed

Monarch and Milkweed

 ## What We Love About This Book

- Beyond the chrysalis — provides a closer look at the Monarch life cycle and the plant that makes it possible

 ## Discover the Book

Monarch and milkweed are made for each other, and their special relationship is the focus of this beautiful picture book. Newcomers and butterfly enthusiasts who are already familiar with the Monarch's annual migration will learn about the biological interdependence of this butterfly and the milkweed plant. The circular structure of the book, beginning with the emergence of one milkweed seedling and ending with another a calendar year later, also presents a complete life cycle of the Monarch. The beginning stages of plant and insect development are presented in parallel on alternating pages up until the moment when the butterfly first feeds on milkweed in full bloom and their stories intertwine.

Readers will appreciate the clear illustrations. The details of the yellow, black, and white Monarch caterpillar; stages of the chrysalis; and mature Monarch are presented in a larger-than-life format. The softly textured pastel and acrylic paintings highlight the close-up biological details, yet also provide panoramic cross-country landscapes in aesthetically pleasing earth tones. Migration routes are found in the book's end pages, with the spring and summer northward migration at the front, and fall and winter southward route represented at the back. An author's note at the back provides further information and lists relevant websites for those who want to learn more.

 ## Explore the Biology

This book tells the twin tales of the milkweed plant and the Monarch butterfly by walking the reader through the life cycle of both insect and plant and illustrating how the two intersect. Perhaps the obvious question is: why do Monarch larvae feed on milkweed? Why not on other plants? The answer is that nature is filled with specialized relationships; some are mutually beneficial and others benefit only one partner. In this case, the Monarch gains at the expense of the milkweed. Milkweed is a common plant that is best known for the role it plays in completing the life cycle of these lovely lepidoptera. Milkweed produces a toxic compound that tastes bitter and discourages insects and large herbivores from consuming it. Monarchs have evolved resistance to this compound, so the larvae use this food source without dying. They are one of the few organisms that can eat this plant; as a result, they have little competition for their food. Even better, the Monarch larvae accumulate the toxin and themselves become poisonous as they mature. This is one of the reasons few birds prey upon this butterfly.

 **Digging Deeper**

Talking Points

1. How are the life cycles of Monarchs and milkweed interrelated?

   After reading the book, ask your readers to describe the stages of the Monarch's life cycle, identifying when it coincides with milkweed's. Find the images in the text that highlight their relationship at different stages; for example, a mature butterfly is shown landing on a milkweed in bloom and sipping nectar; later, a developing Monarch larva is shown feasting on milkweed leaves.

2. Is this a partnership or a one-way relationship?

   Ask the readers if the dynamic between the butterfly and the milkweed is a true partnership or a one-way relationship. In other words, what does the Monarch get from the milkweed and what does the milkweed get from the Monarch? They should come to see that the butterfly is the clear beneficiary in this one-way relationship because the milkweed plant serves as a food source for the developing larvae and produces the toxin that makes the adults bitter and poisonous to eat. The milkweed gains little from the relationship. Monarchs can pollinate milkweed flowers, but so can moths, other butterflies, and bees. What led to the evolution of this relationship is that few insects could eat milkweed, so there was little competition for this food source, and the toxin protected the insect from being eaten.

3. Can Monarchs only eat milkweed?

   Using the images in the book, ask your readers what the larvae feed on (milkweed leaves) and what the adult butterflies eat (nectar from many types of flowers). The adults require a sugar solution to survive, and in nature this is found in nectar-producing flowers and rotting fruit. Since many flowers produce nectar to attract pollinators, adult Monarchs are able to feed upon many different species, ensuring that they can eat throughout their travels, even when milkweed is not in bloom. The larvae, on the other hand, feed only on milkweed.

Related Books

Monarch Butterfly
Written and Illustrated by
Gail Gibbons

Published by Holiday House (1991)
Grade Level: 2-4

. . . .

**An Extraordinary Life: The Story
of a Monarch Butterfly**
Written by Laurence Pringle
Illustrated by Bob Marstall

Published by Orchard Books (1997)
Grade Level: 3-6

. . . .

Are You a Butterfly?
Written by Judy Allen
Illustrated by Tudor Humphries

Published by Kingfisher (2003)
Grade Level: K-3

Learning Experiences

1. **Merge the milkweed and Monarch life cycles.**
   To understand the parallel developmental stages of the Monarch and milkweed, use pictures to represent the seedling-to-seedling and butterfly-to-butterfly progression featured in the book. Have your readers color and cut out the pictures. Using the book as a reference, first order the milkweed pictures on the floor or glue them to a sheet of paper. Next, place the Monarch stages next to the milkweed to show when the two life cycles intersect.

2. **Track the migration.**
   Monarch development and migration is a rich curricular topic, and this multigenerational trek is one of the most beloved natural events in North America. There are many websites that offer up-to-the-minute tracking of the Monarch's migration and videos of metamorphosis. Print a map of North America and, using online resources, draw the various migration routes that Monarchs follow. Depending on reader interest and reading levels, the map can be as simple as the one shown on the end pages of the book, or can be made more complex by adding layers of detail such as migration dates, generations, speed, and specific locations en route.

3. **Plant a Monarch way station.**
   As Monarchs make their journey north and south each year, they must find stops along the way to refuel and reproduce. Create a way-station habitat that provides for all the Monarch's needs, including nectar plants for adults, milkweed for larvae, nearby structures for chrysalis attachment, dark stones for warming in the sun, and puddles for water. Your habitat can be planted directly in the ground, in raised beds, or in containers. In addition to providing a temporary home for Monarchs, your new butterfly habitat will provide the perfect location for observers.

The Life Cycle of the Monarch Butterfly and Milkweed Plant

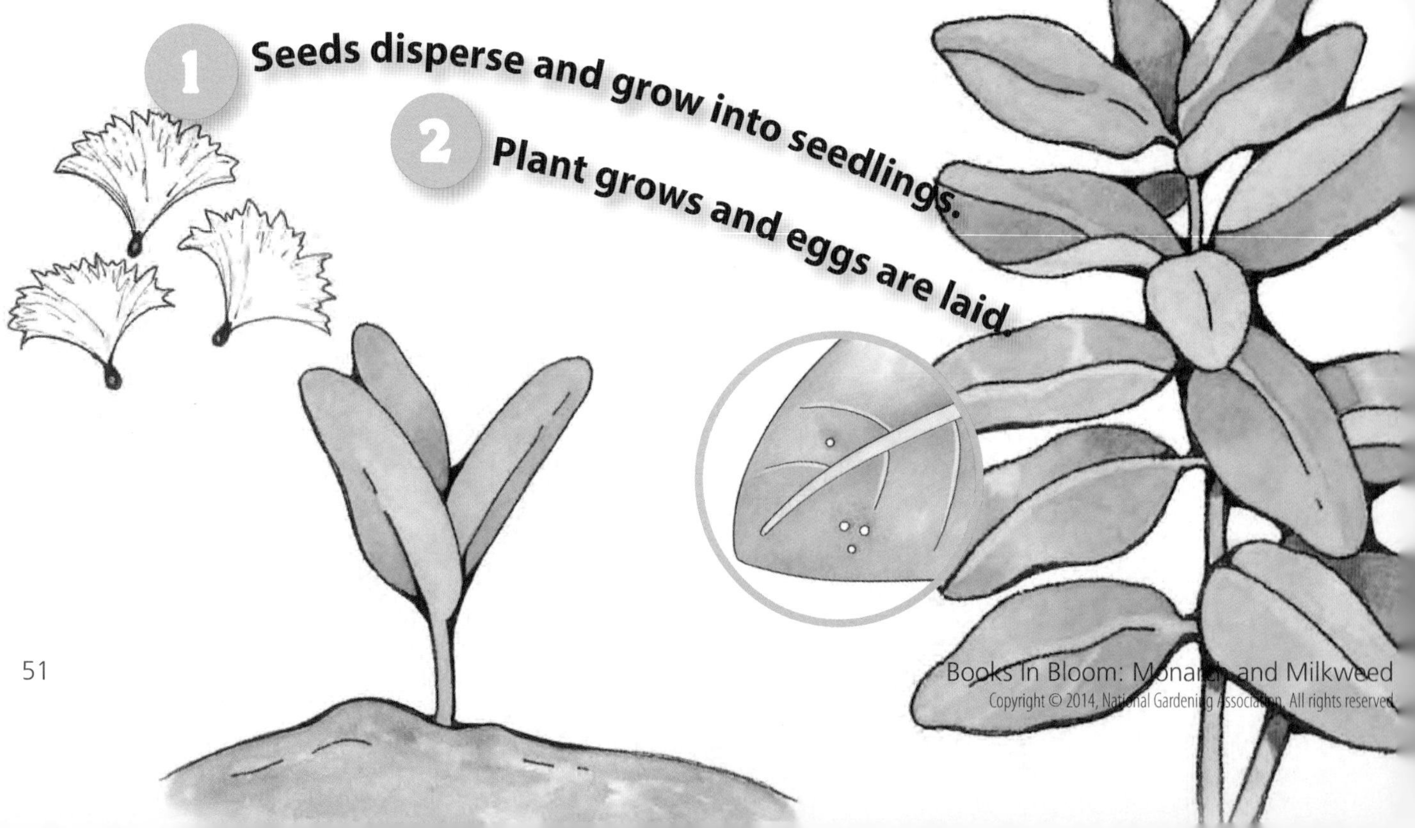

1 Seeds disperse and grow into seedlings.

2 Plant grows and eggs are laid.

Monarch Migration Map

Objective	To explore the journey of the Monarch butterflies.
Time	8 to 10 weeks
Materials	• Map of North America • Milkweed plants or seeds • Monarch observation worksheet
Laying the Groundwork	Ask readers: • **What is the life cycle of a butterfly?** (Butterflies go through many changes during their lives. A butterfly starts as a small egg, which then hatches into a caterpillar. This caterpillar then feeds on plant leaves and grows. When it reaches a certain size, it builds a chrysalis around itself. Even though it may look like it is dormant and in a sleeping bag, the developing butterfly is busy forming its wings within this structure. In the last stage of its life, the butterfly emerges from its chrysalis and takes flight. It eats nectar and pollen from flowers and lays eggs to complete the life cycle. Butterflies lay their eggs on plants that caterpillars like to eat so that as soon as the young hatch, they can begin growing.) • **What is migration?** (Migration refers to the movement of animals, usually seasonal, to find food or more favorable environmental conditions. Monarchs move south each fall to escape cold temperatures and north each spring to find additional food sources.)

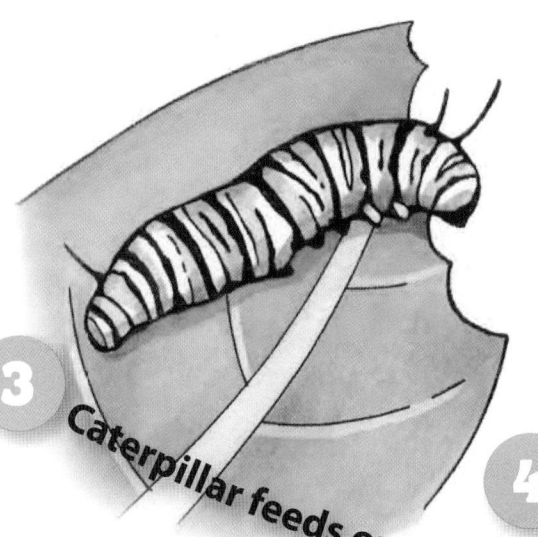

3 Caterpillar feeds on growing leaves.

4 Chrysalis forms.

5 Plant flowers and butterflies emerge.

Exploration

1. Using a map of North America, discuss the migration routes that Monarchs follow.

2. Add dates indicating approximately when the Monarchs first reach each stage in their journey to your map, using data submitted to the citizen science project Journey North at *www.learner.org/jnorth/monarch/*.
Data is available from 1997 to the present.

3. Brainstorm with your readers the reasons that the dates would vary each year.
Temperatures and food availability should top the list.

4. Begin observation in your outdoor space.
Plant milkweed plants in containers, in raised beds, or in the ground and observe regularly. Record temperatures for each day and note how many Monarchs are observed. You can share this data online through the Journey North website with other observers across the country.

Branching Out Ask students to pretend they are Monarch butterflies and have them write a diary about their journey. Make sure they understand that an individual butterfly does not survive to fly all the way north and back each year, but rather, multiple generations make the journey.

NAME _____   DATE _____

Monarch Migration Map

Date	Temperature		Number of Monarchs Observed
	High	Low	

Date	Temperature		Number of Monarchs Observed
	High	Low	

NAME   DATE

Life Cycle Stages of the Monarch Butterfly and Milkweed Plant

PICK, PULL, SNAP!

Where Once a Flower Bloomed

BY LOLA M. SCHAEFER

ILLUSTRATED BY LINDSAY BARRETT GEORGE

Written by Lola M. Schaefer
Illustrated by Lindsay Barrett George

• • • • • • •

Published by Greenwillow Books (2003)
Grade Level: 1-4

Pick, Pull, Snap! Where Once a Flower Bloomed

 ## What We Love About This Book

- Infectiously cheerful color choices
- Seasonal examples that reinforce the core concept
- Flower cross-sections that allow readers to see how fruit develops

 ## Discover the Book

The combination of ingenious book design, appealing illustrations, and carefully crafted text makes this book a powerhouse of information about the biological link between flower and fruit. The developmental progression, from flower to fruit, of six plants — peas, raspberries, corn, peaches, peanuts, and pumpkin — is presented. The engaging text highlights each plant's preferred growing location, explains how the pollen travels, and shows the sequence of growth from blossom to fruit, always ending with the reminder that the fruit is found "where once a flower bloomed."

Botanical details are accurately rendered in the lifelike gouache paintings, which include a glimpse of the full-grown plant, a cross-section of the flower, and a close-up of the mature fruit. The gatefolds present stunning triple-page panoramic views featuring children harvesting each fruit with a "pick," "pull," or "snap." Illustrator Lindsay Barrett George uses pastel-colored backgrounds to emphasize the plants and plant parts in close-up views.

 ## Explore the Biology

Most young readers are familiar with flower and fruit diversity, but helping readers connect the two is where this book really shines. Flowers develop into fruits following pollination. However, to the untrained observer, it is not always apparent that the shape of the flower determines the shape of the fruit. With flower cross-sections, readers are shown the internal workings of the corn, peanut, peach, pea, raspberry, and pumpkin flower followed by an illustration of the developing fruit. Special attention is given to the ovule, the structure that will eventually form the seed, so that the reader can visualize where the seed forms and how it is ultimately encased in or attached to the fruit. The author chose the six examples wisely, because their flowers and fruits are dramatically different — even their pollination strategies vary (wind, bee, or self-pollination). What makes this book so much fun is that the reader gets to visually superimpose the flower cross-section onto the fruit.

 **Digging Deeper**

Talking Points

1. How does the flower develop into a fruit?

As you go through the book, call attention to each flower and ask your readers to describe it. Next, describe the fruit that the flower forms. As you move from plant to plant, ask how the flowers differ and how these differences are reflected in the fruits.

2. How does the shape of the flower influence who pollinates it?

Ask readers to notice how the flower shapes of the plants differ. Floral diversity reflects evolutionary history; because species have adapted different pollination and seed dispersal strategies, they have different flowers. Using the book as a guide, make a chart that lists each of the six plants, its pollinator, and the visual clues in the illustrations that help you identify the pollinating mechanism — wind, bee, or self-pollination.

After completing the chart, you may notice that in the book, bumblebees pollinate both raspberry plants and pumpkins. Many insects (and there are literally tens of thousands of different species) are generalists like the bumblebee, whereas others are specialists and visit only one or a few flower types. The relationship between floral structure and pollinator is one of the most fascinating examples of coevolution — the process by which two species that mutually benefit from their relationship evolve together. In this case, insects get food — nectar and pollen — while the plant gets its pollen carried to another flower. Since bees tend to visit one species at a time, in this case, the raspberry or pumpkin, they help ensure that the pollen is delivered to the right flower. Both win.

3. What's different about wind-pollinated flowers?

Identify a flower in the text that is pollinated by the wind. For example, corn, like many other grasses, is wind-pollinated. Ask your readers to compare the corn flower to one that is bee-pollinated, such as the raspberry or pumpkin. How do they differ? Insect-pollinated flowers use smell, shape, and color to communicate with their insect partner. On the other hand, wind-pollinated flowers do not need to communicate with the wind, so they tend to be odorless, less showy, and green. Their challenge is to "catch" the pollen as it drifts by. In corn, "wind waves golden tassels" and carries the pollen away from this male flower. The female flower, the ear, catches the pollen using its long and thread-like silks (the stigma and style of this flower). Each silk connects to an ovule with a single egg, and each pollen grain grows a single cell down the entire length of the silk to fertilize this egg.

Flower Cross Section

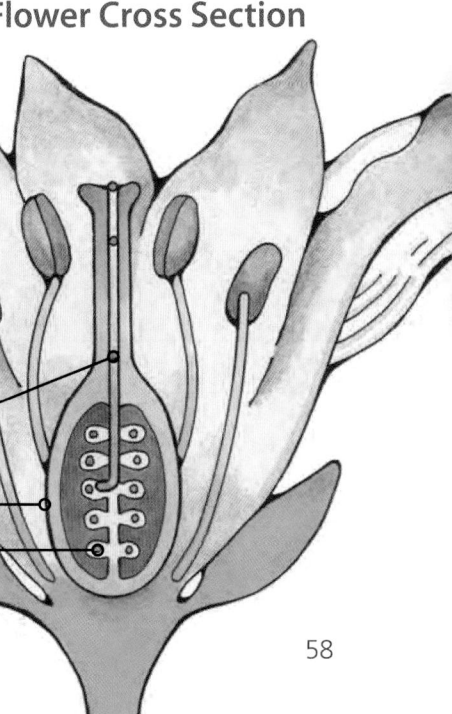

Pollen with sperm
Ovary becomes the fruit
Ovule (forms the seed)

Related Books

The Reason for a Flower
Written and Illustrated by Ruth Heller

Published by Puffin Press (1999)
Grade Level: preK-3

· · · · · · · ·

Monarch and Milkweed (p.48)
Written by Helen Frost
Illustrated by Leonid Gore

Published by Atheneum Books
for Young Readers (2008)
Grade Level: K-3

Learning Experiences

1. Explore what's inside a fruit.

Apple prints provide the perfect way for students to study cross-sections of fruit and identify seeds. Cut an apple longitudinally to show the seeds. Make prints by dipping fruit halves in paint and then stamping them on paper. Make a print on the far right side of a page; when that is dry, on the far left side, sketch the mature flower to reinforce the concept that the flower becomes the fruit. Challenge your readers to sketch their ideas about the intermediate stages of the flower-to-fruit transformation. After this experience, invite them to look again at the cross-section of the flowers on the book's flap pages and ask them to identify which part of the flower becomes the fruit.

2. Be a fruit detective.

In the fall or spring, follow the course of a flowering plant in your neighborhood by keeping a journal. Use a digital camera to record the progression from flower to fruit — weekly photos will probably work for most plants. Based on the shape of the flower, predict what the fruit will look like. Since the primary function of fruit is to disperse seeds, predict how this fruit will disperse its seeds.

3. Identify the fruits in the book.

In a flowering plant, the tissues surrounding the seeds are the fruit. Using this information, first ask your readers to identify what surrounds the seeds for each of the plants. Sometimes the fruit is obvious, as in the case of the peach or raspberry, and other times it is not so clear. For example, the shell that surrounds peanut seeds is the fruit and is inedible. The corn kernel is tricky. The fruit, in this case, is actually fused to the seed so that the seed and fruit appear as one structure. See the table below for details about each featured fruit. After having your readers identify all the fruits, determine whether they are all edible.

Plant	Fruit	Edible?
Pea	Outer shell	Yes
Raspberry	Berry	Yes
Corn	Outer layer surrounding kernel	Yes
Peach	Skin, flesh, pit	Skin and flesh are edible; pit is not edible
Peanut	Shell (the separate papery structure surrounding each peanut is the seed coat and not part of the fruit)	Fruit is not edible; seed and seed coat are edible
Pumpkin	Skin, orange flesh, strings	Yes

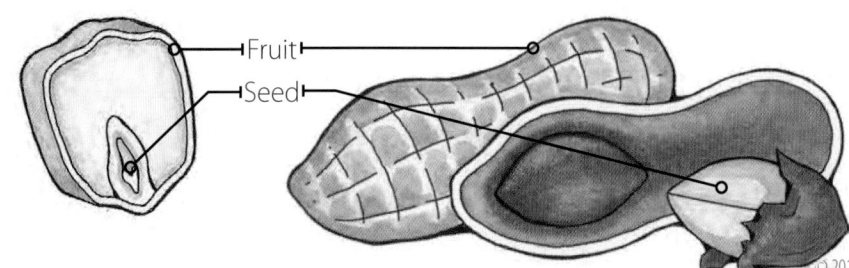

Books In Bloom: Lesson

Flower Shape

Objective	To explore the relationship between flower shape, pollination, and fruit development.
Time	1 hour
Materials	• Flower, fruit, and pollinator pictures • Chart paper • Markers
Laying the Groundwork	Ask readers: • Do all flowers look the same? What are some of the ways they are different? (Flowers vary greatly in size, shape, color, and pattern.) • Why do you think flowers look different from each other? (Some flowers need help from special animals called pollinators to make their seeds; by looking different, they can compete for the attention of different pollinators. Others pollinate themselves or use the wind.)

Progression of Apple Flower to Fruit

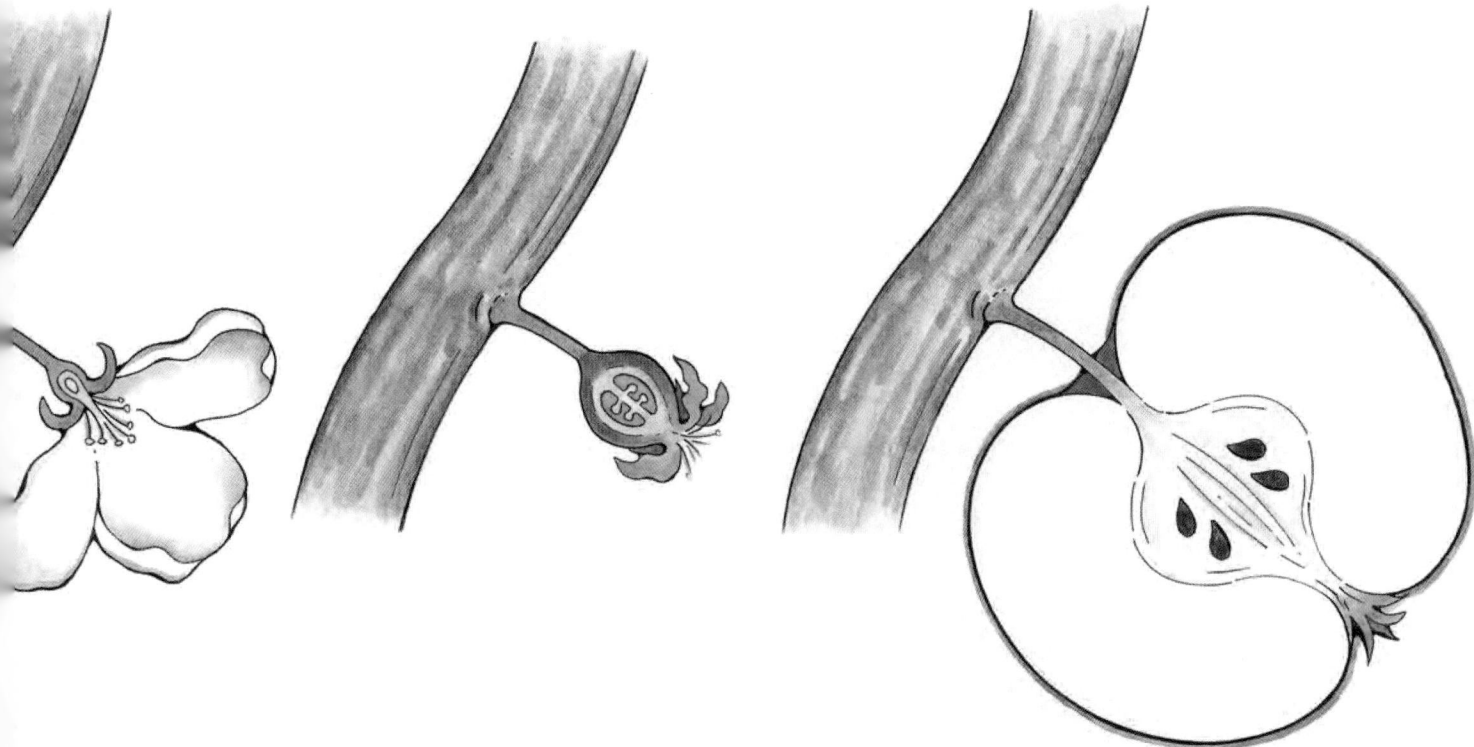

Exploration:

1. Share with readers that the relationship between flower structure and pollinator is one of the most fascinating examples of coevolution — the process by which two species that mutually benefit from their relationship evolve together. In this case, insects get food — nectar and pollen — while the plant gets its pollen carried to another flower.

2. Using the flower, fruit, and pollinator pictures, ask readers to notice how the flower shapes of each plant differ.

3. Make a table that lists each of the six plants, its pollinator, and the visual clues in the illustrations that help you identify the pollinating mechanism — wind, bee, or self-pollination.

4. After completing the chart, you may notice that bumblebees pollinate both raspberry plants and pumpkins.

   Many insects (and there are literally tens of thousands of different species) are generalists like the bumblebee, while others are specialists and visit only one or a few flower types. Even though they can visit many different types of flowers, specialists tend to visit only one at a time, to ensure that the pollen is delivered to the right flower.

5. If possible, visit a school or community garden to watch pollinators in action.

   Ask readers to make observations in a journal and discuss their observations when they return.

Branching Out Have readers design their own flower. They should include details about how it is pollinated and draw a picture of what the resulting fruit would look like.

NAME   DATE

Flower Shape

Flower	Fruit	Pollinator
Pea Flower		
Raspberry Flower		
Corn Flowers (ear [female] and tassels [male])		
Peach Flower		
Peanut Flower		
Pumpkin Flower		

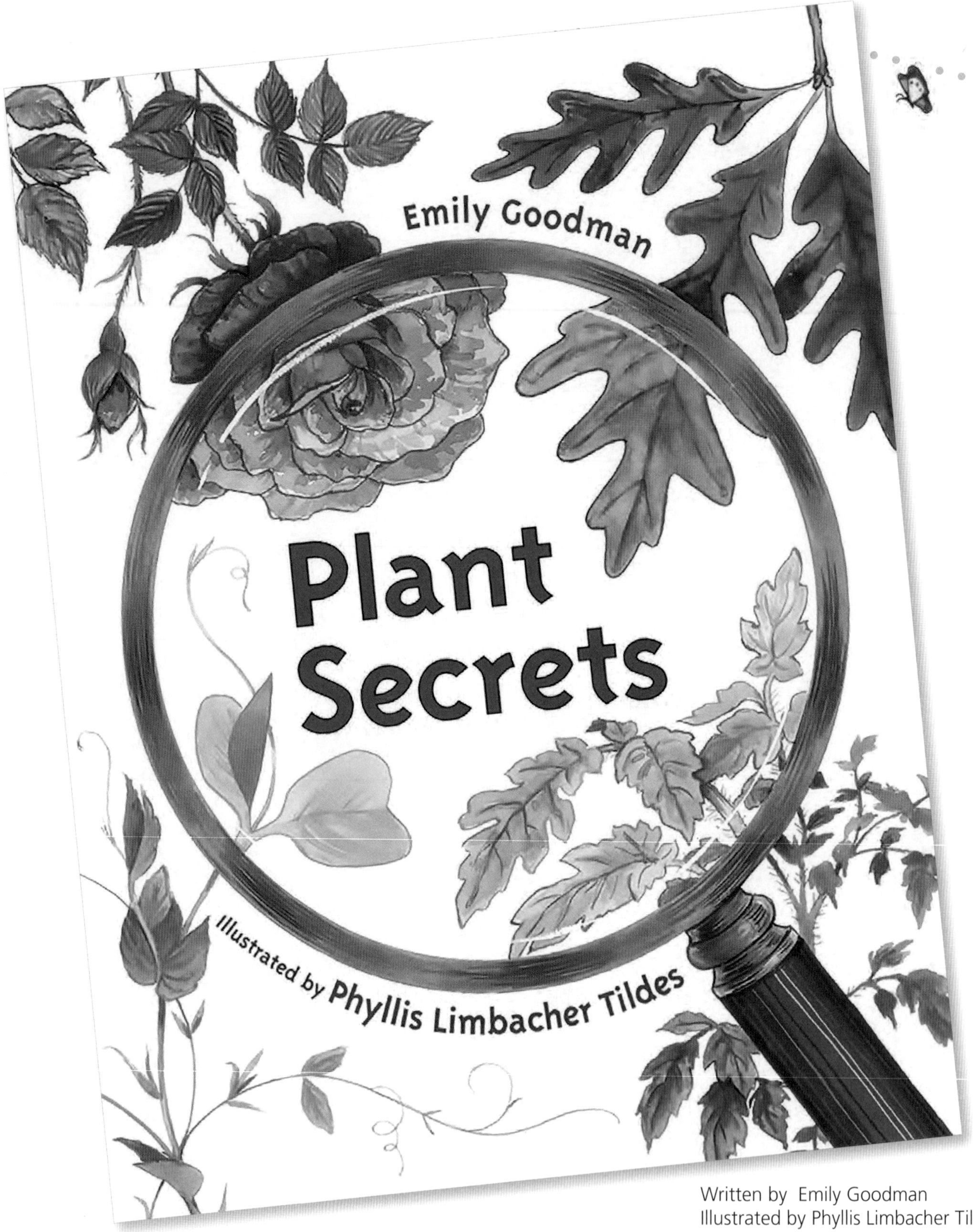

Emily Goodman

Plant Secrets

Illustrated by Phyllis Limbacher Tildes

Written by Emily Goodman
Illustrated by Phyllis Limbacher Tildes

Published by Charlesbridge (2009)
Grade Level: K-2

Plant Secrets

What We Love About This Book

• Engaging presentation of the life cycle of four familiar plants

Discover the Book

Plant Secrets does a masterful job of conveying both differences in plants and similarities in plant life cycles in an accurate and entertaining manner. As promised by the enticing title, this book is structured around four "secrets" that reveal stages of the plant's life cycle. Goodman and Tildes use comparative terms and imagery to help readers visualize a well-chosen quartet of main characters: the pea, rose, oak, and tomato, as they cycle through the stages of seed, plant, flower, fruit, and back to seed. The text features comparisons with familiar things, such as "round like a plate," "shorter than a cat," and "taller than a person," to help young readers grasp the size and shape of various plants; stars, bells, feathers, and "balls of fuzz" describe what flowers look like. Readers will enjoy the details on the illustrated seed packets, featuring descriptions like "prize-winning" and "guaranteed to grow."

What makes this an engaging book to read with children is the clever ways that Goodman and Tildes invite readers to interact with the content. They establish a pattern: a dilemma is introduced, the "secret" is revealed, and details are offered. Children will quickly recognize the symbolic magnifying glass announcing the next secret. Questions invite reader participation, and even the endpapers offer a flower name quiz. The book concludes with each of the showcased plants pictured in the stage in which we know it best: the pea as seed, the oak as tree, the rose as flower, and the tomato as fruit.

Explore the Biology

The plant kingdom is incredibly diverse, yet plants by definition share many features. It is this concept that Plant Secrets so wonderfully conveys, by taking readers through the milestones of one generation of a flowering plan — or, as plant biologists say, "from seed to seed" — by revealing the commonalities of plant development through four secrets. These secrets, below, accurately describe foundational ideas in plant biology, are reinforced by the realistic illustrations, and can form the basis for any curriculum about plants.

Secret 1: "Hidden inside each seed is a tiny new plant."

Seeds carry an embryo, typically dormant, as well as a food source (sort of like a trust fund) from the mother plant that helps the emerging seedling establish its first roots, shoots, and leaves. The genius of seeds is that through dormancy, the embryo can coordinate its growth with the seasons and proper growing conditions.

Secret 2: "Plants can grow flowers."

Flowers are reproductive structures that produce the plant's sperm (carried in pollen) and eggs (housed in the floral ovaries) and facilitate fertilization. Flower diversity is a result of adaptations developed to ensure pollination.

Secret 3: "Hidden inside each flower are parts that can make a fruit."

Flowers are the precursors to fruit; hence, fruit diversity is a function of floral diversity. It is primarily the position of the flower's ovary that determines what the fruit will look like.

Secret 4: "Hidden inside fruits are seeds."

Readers may wonder how the seeds get inside the fruit. Because the embryo developed inside the flower, which then transformed into the fruit, the seeds ultimately reside in the fruit.

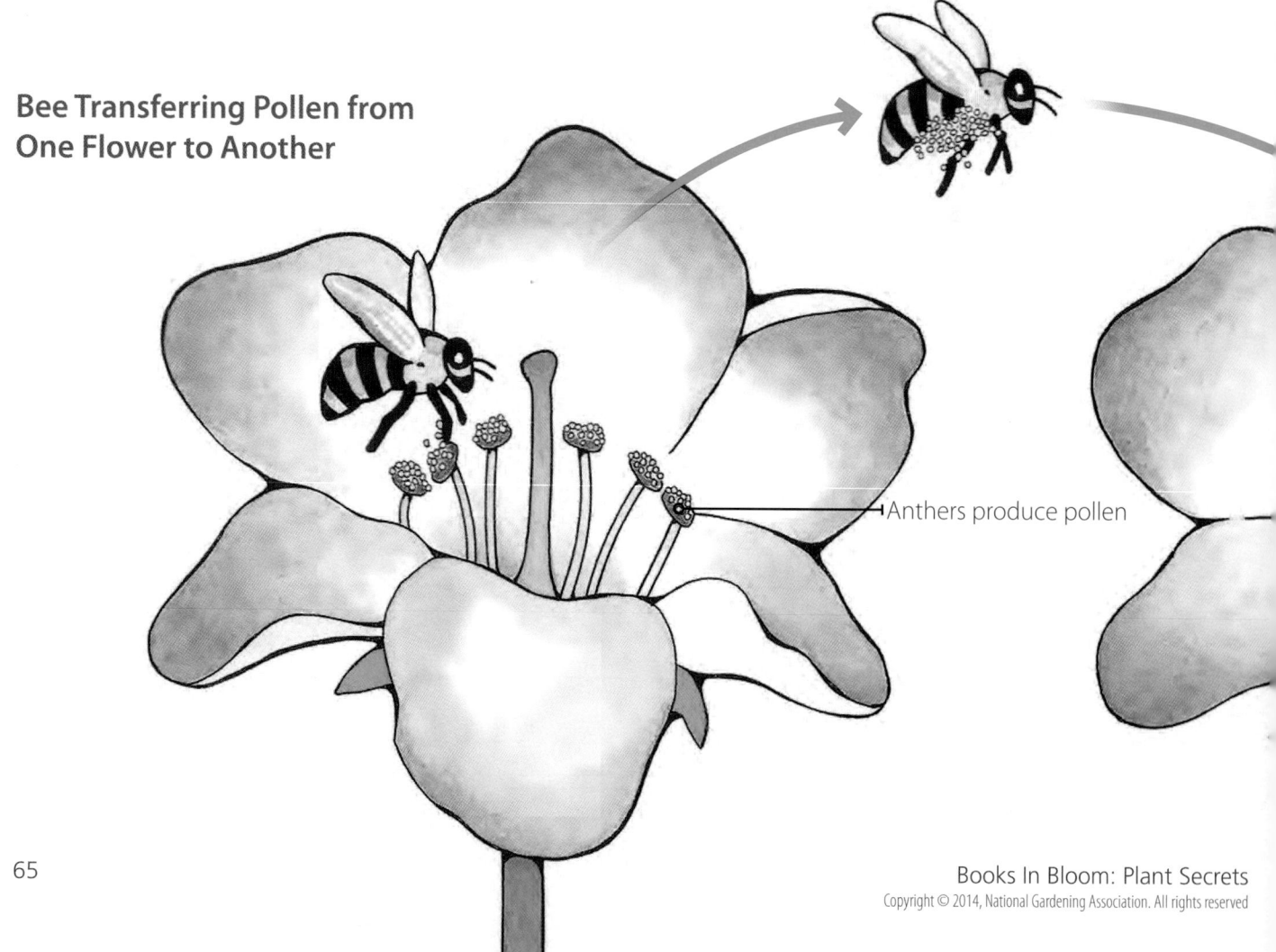

Bee Transferring Pollen from One Flower to Another

Anthers produce pollen

Digging Deeper

Talking Points

1. **If plants have the same secrets, why do they look different?**
   The four secrets tell the readers that seeds, flowers, or fruits of all plants have the same function even though they look very different. The differences are adaptations of plants to their environment developed to ensure their survival.

2. **Why are seeds inside fruit, and what's the purpose of fruit?**
   Fruit develops from the parts of the flower that encase the developing seeds. For this reason, the seeds ultimately end up inside the fruit. The purpose of having seeds inside fruit is to help disperse the seeds. Have your readers examine the page with the text "Next come fruits," and have them describe any differences they observe. Ask them why they think the fruits are so different if they all have the same secret—"hidden inside fruits are seeds." Lead them to the realization that the type of fruit reflects how the plant spreads its seeds.

Fruit Characteristics	Method of Travel	Example
Fur hooks or barbs	Sticking to animal.	Burdock
Bright color, tasty	Being eaten by bird or other animal and excreted.	Cherry, Tomato
Fluff or "parachutes"	Being carried by wind.	Dandelion, cattail
Can float	Drifting on water.	Coconut
Bursts open	Is flung from parent.	Touch-Me Not, Pansy

3. **How do familiar words help us describe the unfamiliar?**
   In Plant Secrets, the author uses comparisons to help us understand the size and shape of plants or leaves. For example, she uses "narrow as needles," "round as a plate," and shaped like a "star." Bring in a variety of leaves and ask each child to choose one. Challenge them to use familiar terms as the author does to help others recognize its features. Put all the leaves in the middle of a circle and organize a game of "I Spy." A player might say, "I spy a leaf that is orange like a pumpkin and pointy like a star."

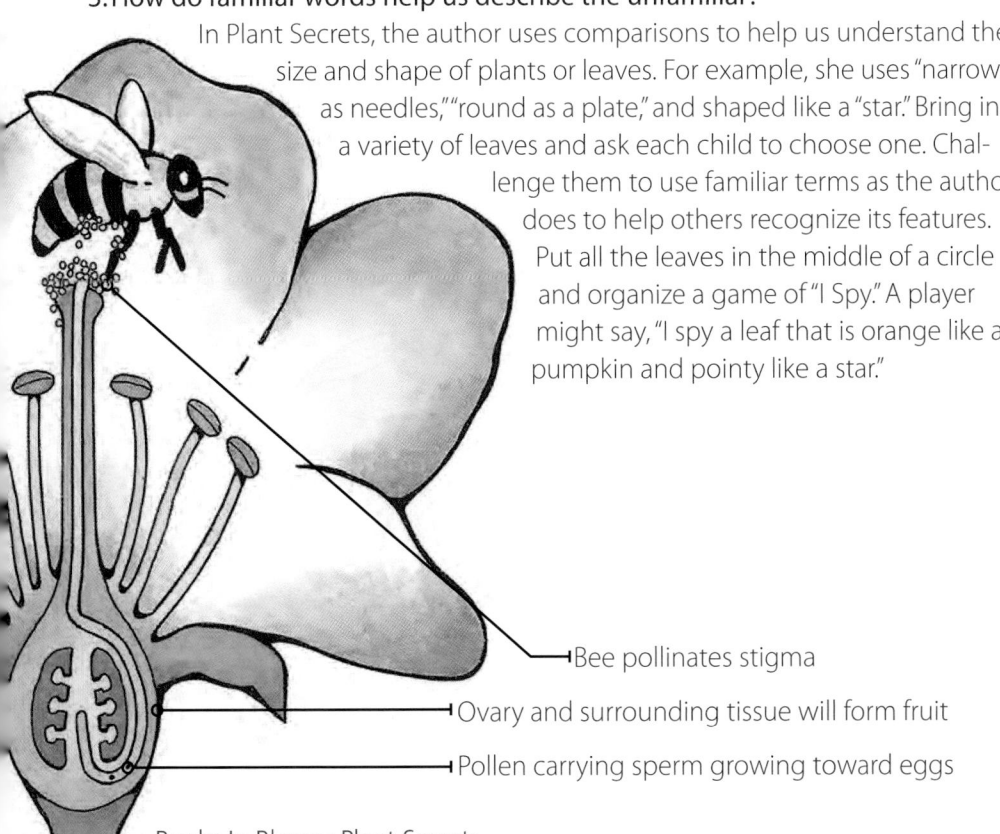

Bee pollinates stigma

Ovary and surrounding tissue will form fruit

Pollen carrying sperm growing toward eggs

Books In Bloom: Plant Secrets

Related Books

A Fruit Is a Suitcase for Seeds (p.1)
Written by Jean Richards
Illustrated by Anca Hariton

Published by The Millbrook Press (2002)
Grade Level: K-2

• • • • • • • •

A Seed Is Sleepy
Written by Dianna Hutts Aston
Illustrated by Sylvia Long

Published by Chronicle Books (2007)
Grade Level: K-5

Learning Experiences

1. Make life-cycle drawings.
Before reading the book, give each child a piece of paper folded into fourths. Ask them to draw a pea, rose, oak, and tomato, one in each quarter. As you read the book, have them identify which stage of the life cycle is represented by their drawing. Next, ask them to again fold a piece of paper in fourths, and this time to pick one of the four "main characters" from the book (a pea, rose, oak, or tomato) and draw and label each of its secrets (or stages) sequentially.

2. Investigate your state flower, fruit, and seed.
Your state probably does not have an official fruit or seed, but it does have an official state flower. Have your readers draw their state flower, followed by the fruit it develops into with the seeds placed inside it. One exception: if you live in Maine, your state flower (the pinecone) is not actually a flower (sorry). Some plants, called gymnosperms, like pine trees, do not produce seeds in flowers, but instead produce seeds in cone-like structures.

3. Grow plants from seed to seed.
Plants such as beans, marigolds, and mustards are easy to grow and develop quickly, offering readers a firsthand experience with a plant's life cycle "from seed to seed."

Germinating Corn Kernel

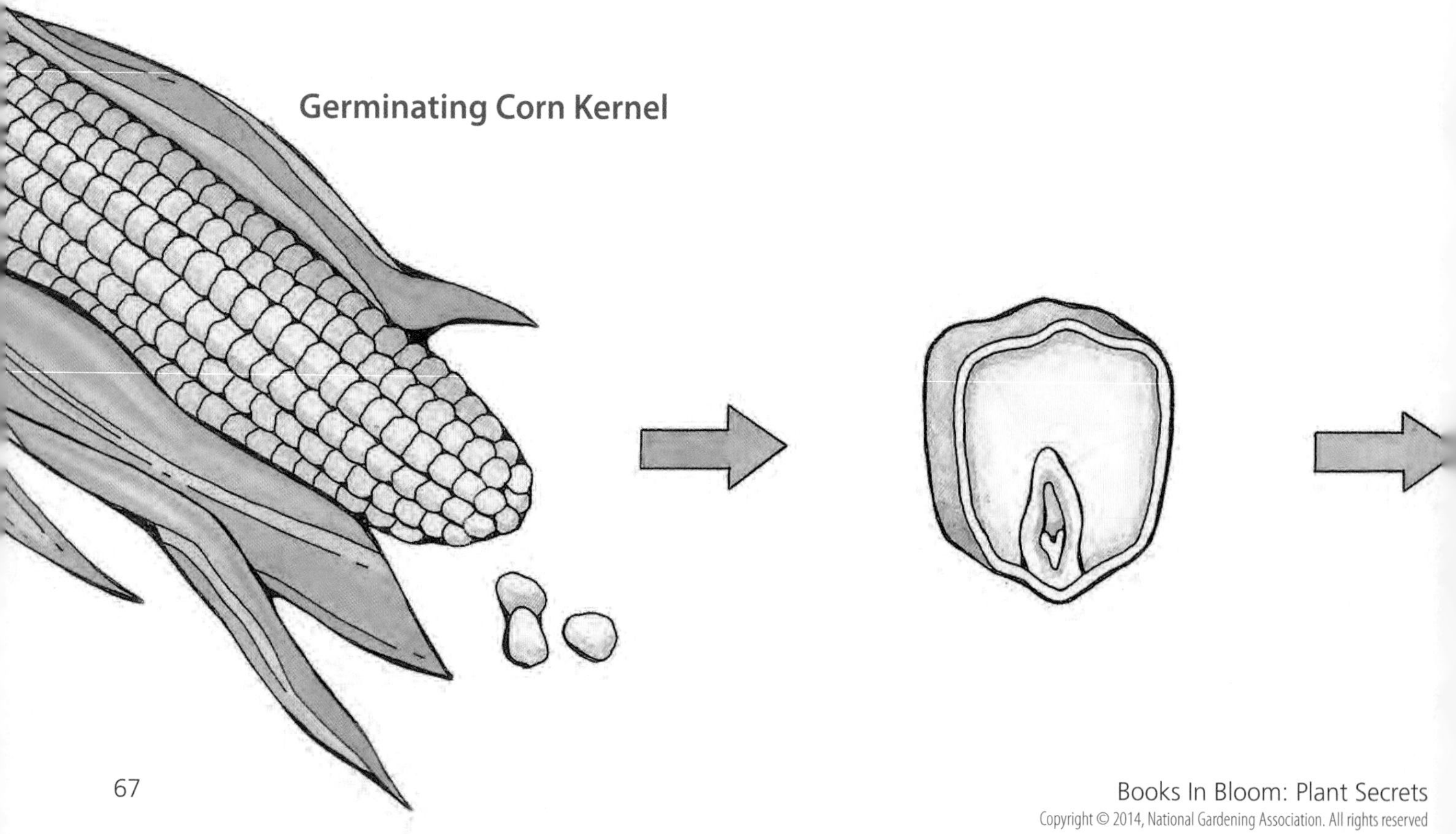

 **Lesson Plan**

From Seed to Seed

Objective   To demonstrate each stage in a plant's life cycle.

Time   6 to 8 weeks

Materials
- Seeds from fast-growing plants, such as beans, marigolds, or mustards, from a seller such as Wisconsin Fast Plants (*www.fastplants.org*)
- Potting soil mix
- At least 3 or 4 4-inch pots or plastic cups with holes punched in the bottom
- Journals
- Crayons
- Rulers
- Plant Growth Chart

Laying the Groundwork

Ask readers:
- **How do people change during their lives?**
  (We begin as babies, grow into toddlers, then young children, then teenagers, and eventually adults; adults have more babies.)

- **How do plants change during their lives?**
  (They start out as seeds, then become seedlings, then full-grown plants. Once they are mature, they produce flowers, which produce fruit and seeds to make more plants)

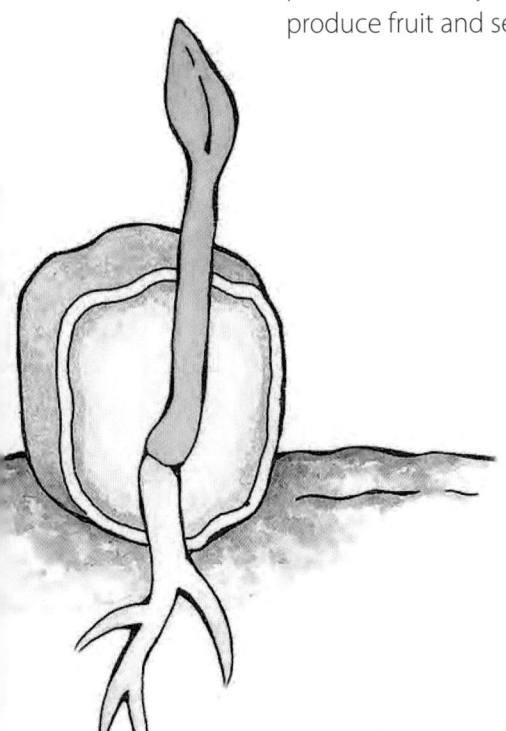

Exploration

1. **Plant seeds indoors following these steps:**
   - Use 4-inch pots with drainage holes. Alternatively, use plastic drinking cups with holes punched in the bottom. If using clear cups, plant seeds on the side of the container to watch root growth too.
   - Fill the containers with a lightweight soilless potting mix. Moisten the soil before placing it in containers. These mixes allow good drainage, providing both the aeration and the moisture seedlings need. Readers can experiment with different types of growing media and observe the growth rates.
   - Plant seeds according to the instructions on the packets. If you do not see instructions about how deep to plant your seeds, a simple rule is to plant them 1 ½ to 2 times as deep as the width of the seed. Place pots or cups in a tray to catch excess water, then mist using a spray bottle.
   - Place trays in a location that receives 6 to 8 hours of direct sunlight or under fluorescent lights for 12 to 14 hours per day. Most seeds germinate best in warm and humid conditions.
   - Check daily to make sure the mix is moist. With the right conditions, most garden seeds should germinate in 7 to 14 days (unless otherwise noted on the seed packet).

2. **Once seeds sprout, begin to track growth using the Plant Growth Chart.**
   Ask readers to record height, identify the life-cycle stage (e.g., seed, seedling, mature plant), and describe growth in either words or illustrations.

3. **When seeds form, review the cycle together.**
   Ask readers, "How long did each stage last? Were all stages the same length? Do you think this time line would be different for different types of plants?"

Branching Out Experiment with other seeds and compare the life cycles of two different types of plants.

Germinating Peanut Seed

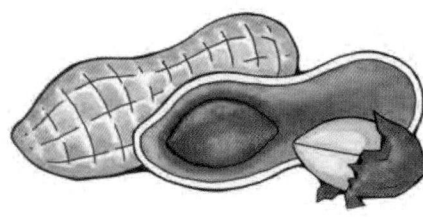  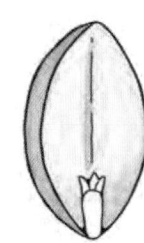  

NAME

DATE

Plant Growth Chart

Plant Name: _____   Date Seeds Planted: _____

Date	Life-cycle Stage	Height	What Does the Plant Look Like?

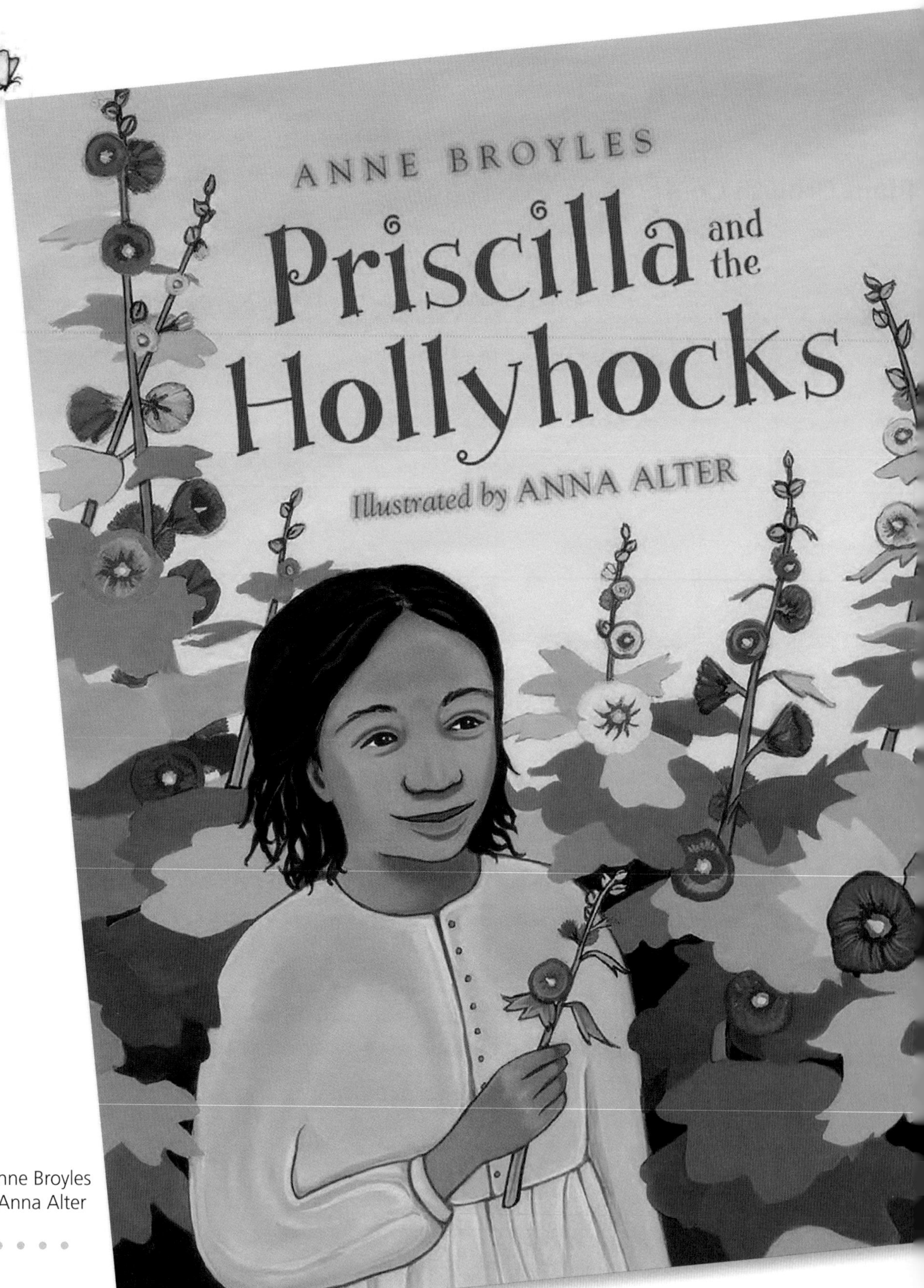

ANNE BROYLES

Priscilla and the Hollyhocks

Illustrated by ANNA ALTER

Written by Anne Broyles
Illustrated by Anna Alter

• • • • • • •

Published by
Charlesbridge (2008)
Grade Level: 3-5

71

Priscilla and the Hollyhocks

What We Love About This Book

- Historical accuracy
- Survival of the human spirit
- Flower as touchstone

Discover the Book

Hollyhock blossoms float through this tragic tale of separation, as Priscilla's mother is sold as a slave to a different plantation during this disturbing era of American history. To console Priscilla, "Old Sylvia" teaches her to make dolls out of hollyhocks like "your ma" did, and floating these on the cow pond becomes her Sunday solace. Priscilla experiences cruelty and indifference at the hand of plantation owners — one white and one Cherokee. When the Cherokees are forced into the infamous Trail of Tears, Priscilla must travel with them. Throughout each transition in her life, Priscilla gathers hollyhock seeds so that they can bloom and grow wherever she is. Basil Silkwood, a historical figure, eventually buys Priscilla's freedom and provides a home for her in Illinois. Broyles presents the last lines as symbolic and literal ones, indicating that Priscilla finally feels "safe," and that she and her beloved hollyhocks can "bloom and grow." The acrylic paintings in flat, saturated, earthy tones convey Priscilla's journey in a folk-art manner.

Although the history and issues surrounding slavery and the Trail of Tears warrant further reading about this complex period in our country's history, Priscilla's tale poignantly showcases the role that a flower can play as a symbol of love and connection in heart-wrenching times. Based on a true story, this book won recognition as a National Council for Social Studies Notable Trade Book and was named a Bank Street College Best Children's Book of the Year.

Explore the Biology

The biology in this book is subtle but important to the story nonetheless. As an enslaved person, Priscilla has few physical possessions, which deprives her of any keepsakes of her family. The hollyhock flower serves as Priscilla's emotional touchstone, perfect in that she can carry seeds with her when she is forced to move. Flowers by their very nature are ephemeral, widely available, and fragile, and these characteristics imbue her dolls. The transformation of the flowers into dolls is a powerful act of the human spirit, making beauty and creating peaceful moments; they may be short-lived but they cannot be taken away, either.

The choice of hollyhock is important to note for several reasons. Hollyhocks are found throughout most of the eastern United States (zones 3-9), enabling Priscilla to take seeds with her from Georgia en route to Illinois. Hollyhocks are easily germinated with minimal soil preparation — they grow best when scattered on the surface of soil and lightly covered — as shown by the author's description of how Priscilla "scattered" and "shook" seeds. Finally, the biennial nature of the plant is recognized by Priscilla — "My hollyhocks sent up tall, green stems, flowered the second spring."

 # Digging Deeper

Talking Points

1. **What was 19th-century America like for Priscilla?**
The setting and context for this complex story require some understanding of the way the 19th-century agrarian economy functioned and was dependent upon slavery. Prepare to offer your readers background information before reading this book. A resource with a strong voice is Kadir Nelson's powerful book, *Heart and Soul: The Story of America and African-Americans*.

2. **What are your touchstones?**
Priscilla used the hollyhock as a way to stay in touch with her past and to find moments of happiness. Ask your readers, when they face difficulties or are away from home, what do they use as a touchstone?

3. **What are biennials?**
The hollyhock is a biennial. Ask readers to list other words with bi as a prefix denoting two, such as bicycle, binary, and bicentennial. As the prefix implies, biennial plants take two growing seasons to complete their life cycle — the first season is dedicated to storing energy, and the second is for reproduction and is when the plant flowers. Flower gardeners know that when growing a biennial, they should not expect flowers until the second season, just as Priscilla does. Ask your readers to name some other biennials. Answers may include carrots, beets, and foxglove.

Learning Experiences

1. Make a hollyhock doll.

Use the directions at the back of *Priscilla and the Hollyhocks* or the directions provided in the included handout to make a hollyhock doll.

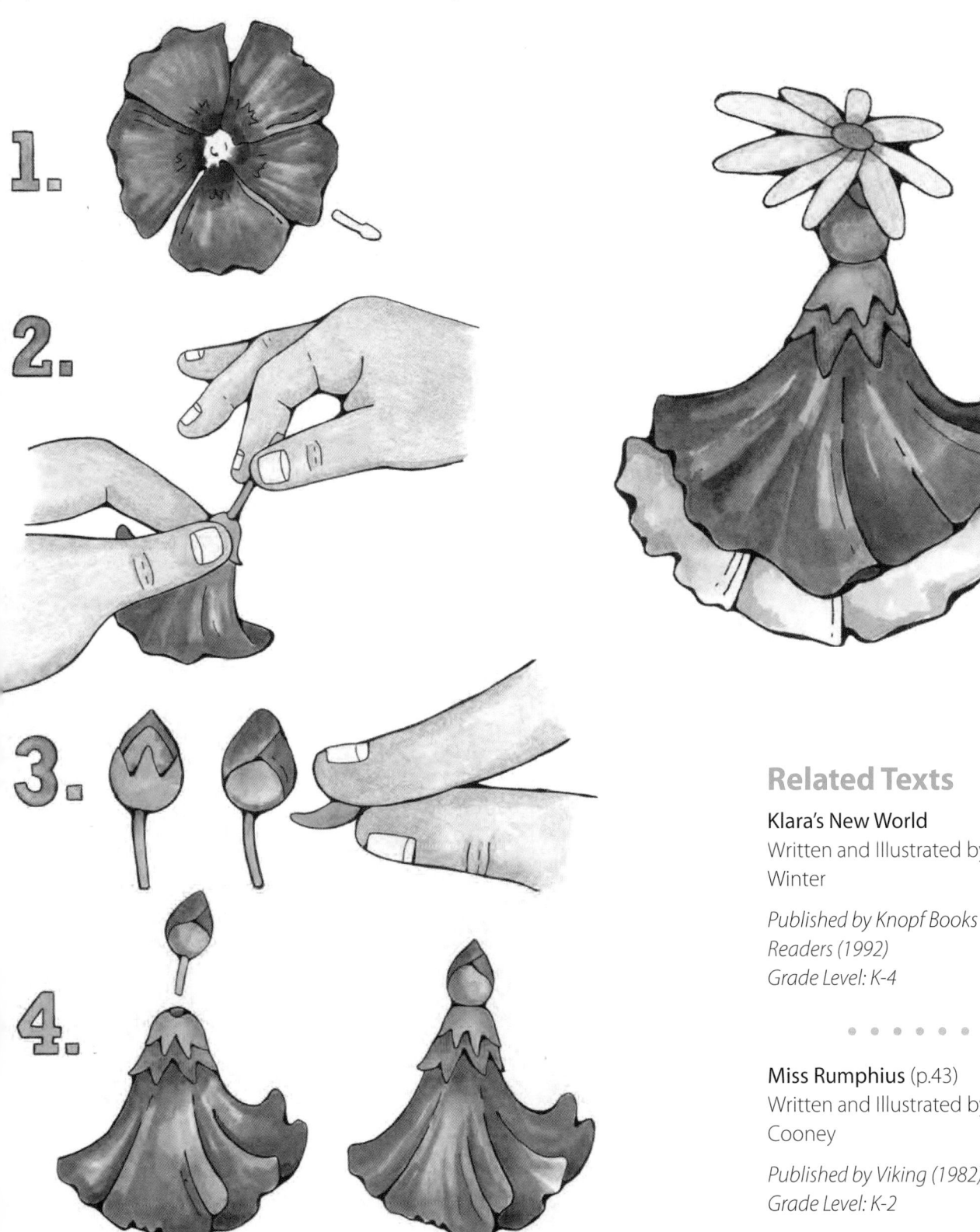

Related Texts

Klara's New World
Written and Illustrated by Jeanette Winter

Published by Knopf Books for Young Readers (1992)
Grade Level: K-4

• • • • • • •

Miss Rumphius (p.43)
Written and Illustrated by Barbara Cooney

Published by Viking (1982)
Grade Level: K-2

2. **Examine flower structures.**

   Making a hollyhock doll provides a nice opportunity to examine floral structures as well as flower development. While preparing the head from a bud, ask your readers to compare the bud to the mature flower. Make a cross-section of a bud by cutting it down the middle with scissors or a knife. Identify all of the floral organs in the mature flower (sepals, petals, stamens, and pistils) and then identify them in the developing bud.

3. **Learn about displacement.**

   To help your readers understand displacement and contextualize the enormity of the Trail of Tears, use online resources to find a U.S. map from the 1830s and then identify the route that the Cherokees were forced to take from Georgia to Oklahoma. Reflecting on Priscilla's repeated displacement, ask your readers to describe what it must have been like for the Cherokee to be forced from their homes.

Flower Parts

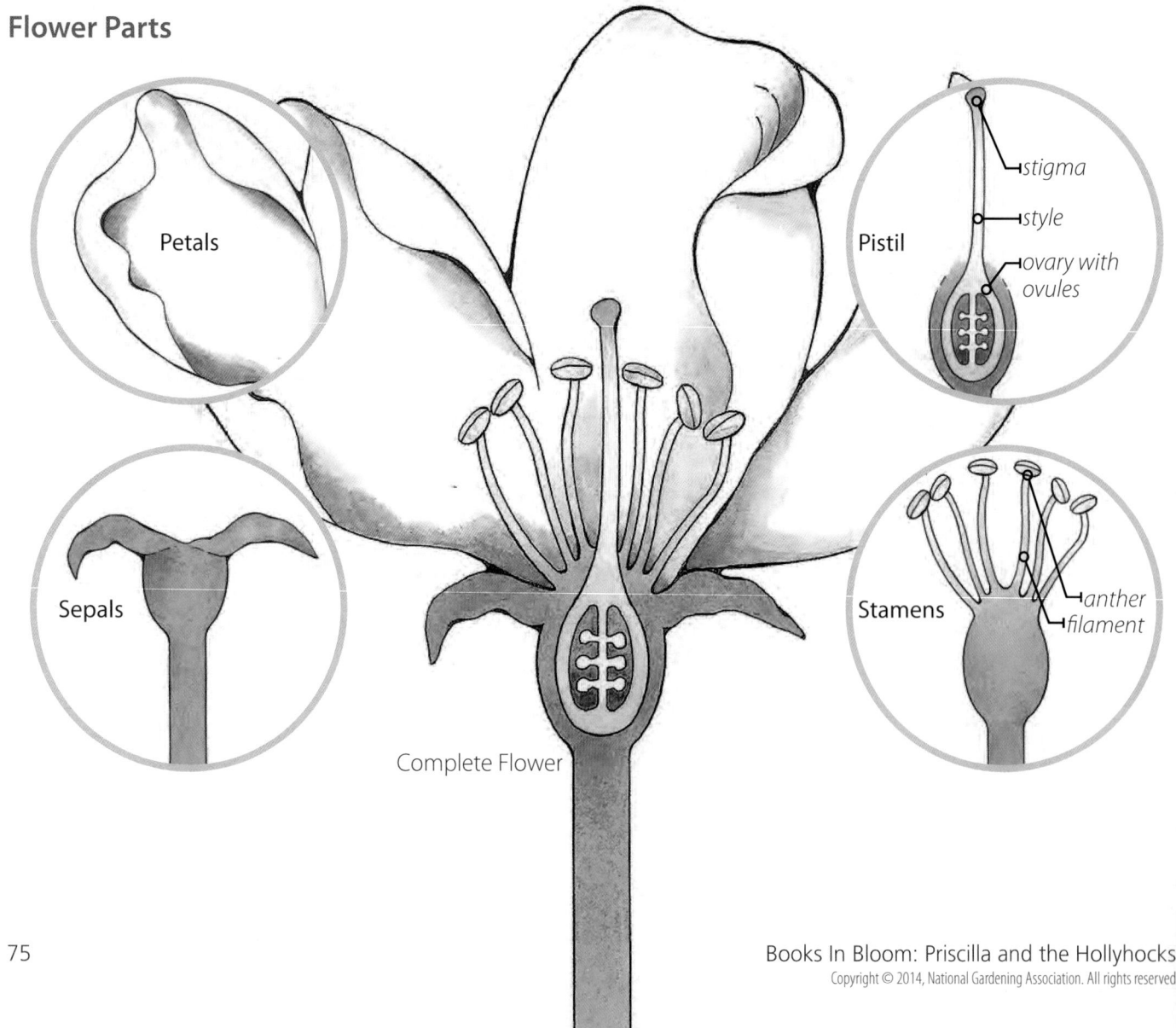

Petals

Pistil

stigma

style

ovary with ovules

Sepals

Stamens

anther

filament

Complete Flower

 **Lesson Plan**

Flowers Up Close*

Objective   To observe and describe various flowers.

Time   1 hour

Materials
- Examples of assorted flowers
  (tulips, lilies, and alstroemeria are easy to dissect and study)
- Hand lenses
- "Flowers Up Close" worksheet
- Craft supplies

Laying the Groundwork

Ask readers:
- **What are some common characteristics of flowers? Why do you think many flowers are colorful and fragrant?**
  (These traits help them attract pollinators.)

- **What is the purpose of a flower?**
  (To facilitate pollination, house the developing seed, and ultimately form the fruit that helps disperse the seed.)

Exploration

1. Pass out flowers to readers and give them a chance to observe them closely with a hand lens.

2. Ask readers to sketch their flower.
   Next, have them split it in half for a better view of its parts and draw a cross-section of their flower. Ask them to write a description of what they see, for example:
   - Eight long, skinny things with flat, dark tops.
   - Six large, heart-shaped, sweet-smelling, soft petals around the outside.

3. Give readers a copy of the "Flowers Up Close" worksheet figure and introduce all the common parts of a flower. Explain that their flower may not look exactly like the one pictured, because not all flowers have all parts. Ask them to compare their flower to the one pictured on the handout.

4. If time and materials allow, have them repeat the steps above with another flower, then compare their findings.

Flowers: Up Close
Answer Key

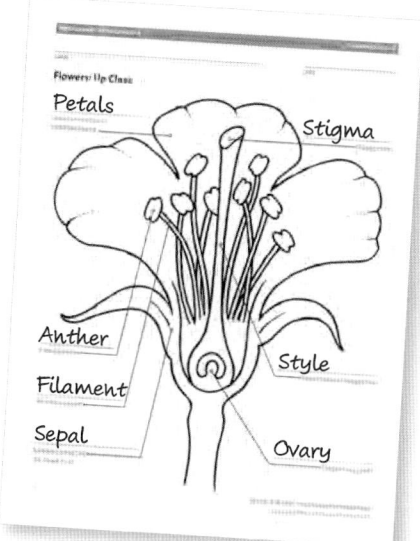

Branching Out   Ask each reader to create his or her own flower using craft materials. Have them include all the basic parts listed on the figure.

*Adapted from GrowLab: Activities for Growing Minds (National Gardening Association, 2009).

NAME   DATE

Flowers: Up Close

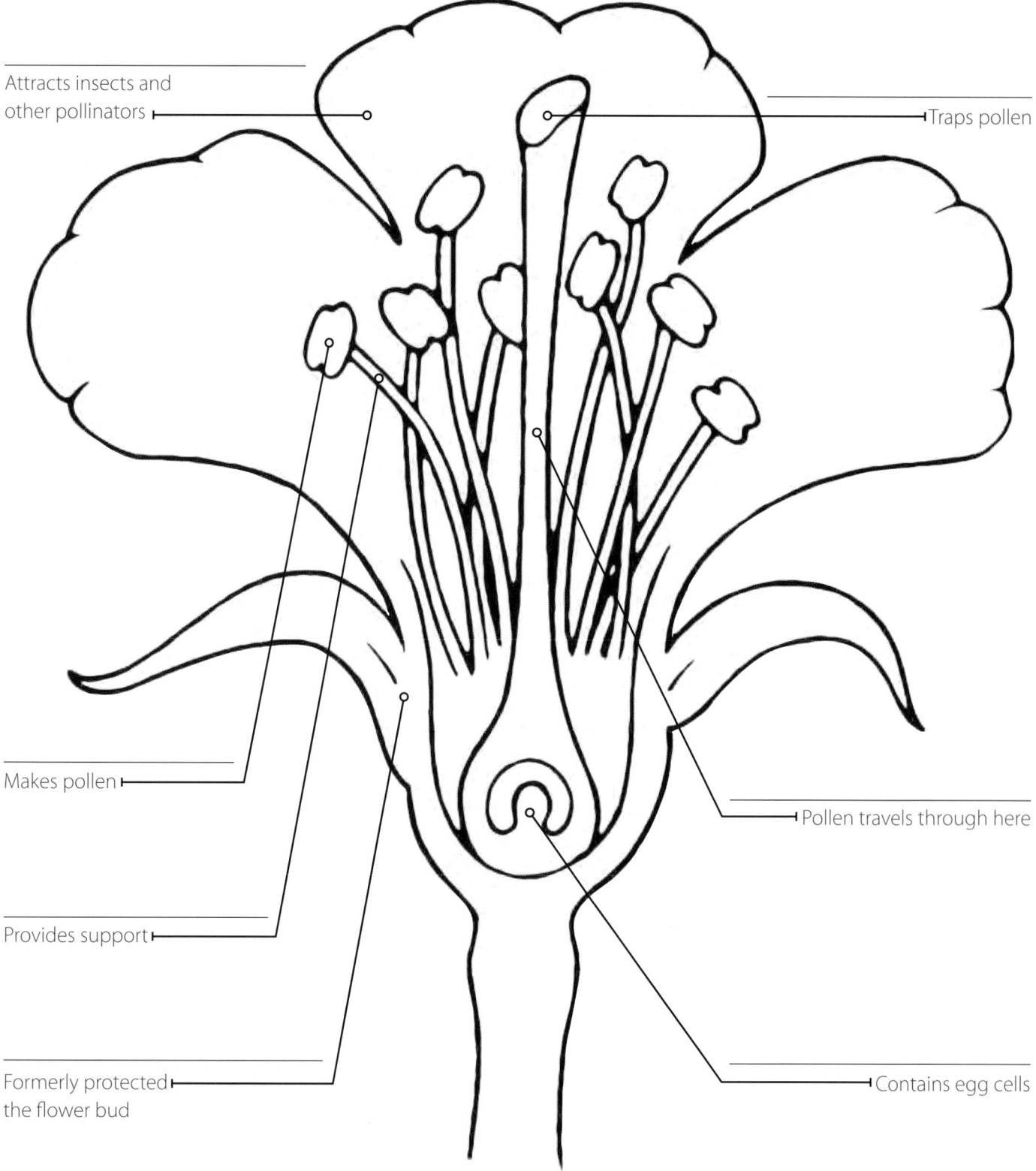

Attracts insects and
other pollinators

Traps pollen

Makes pollen

Pollen travels through here

Provides support

Formerly protected
the flower bud

Contains egg cells

Books In Bloom: Priscilla and the Hollyhocks

By George Levenson
Photographs by Shmuel Thaler

Tricycle Press (2010)
Grade Level: K-4

Pumpkin Circle: The Story of a Garden

K
1
2
3
4

 ## What We Love About This Book

- Stunning photographs
- Image and text synergy
- Linguistic imagery, and sly humor represented by the anonymous pumpkin-orange gloves

 ## Discover the Book

Pumpkin Circle is a strikingly visual, poetic, and informative ride through the life cycle of a pumpkin. As in the video with the same name (on which the book is based), the photographic images and text show that science and poetry can be a powerful and lively combination. The title captures the content perfectly — by learning about the seed-to-seed story of a pumpkin, we also learn the archetypal seed-to-seed "story of a garden."

Poetically speaking, the text is presented through playful font orientation and predictable rhymes such as spring and cling. The hybridization of scientific terms and poetic imagery offers the reader multiple ways of understanding scientific phenomena and appreciating language simultaneously. Photographic details and linguistic metaphor work together seamlessly to present sometimes surprising comparisons; the seeds are described as "reaching down with silky roots, reaching up to dance," while the photograph shows a cross-section of soil with a network of delicate roots and the "dancing" stem with trichomes, or plant hairs. The color palette of strong natural choices — blues, greens, and the requisite orange — enriches the clear biological message.

Nonfiction features abound; close-ups such as trichomes on a stem or five different seed types, scale comparisons (human hands on "huge green leaf"), and sequence boxes provide facts about the life cycle and also show how nonfiction authors convey different types of information. The book concludes with a page jam-packed with directions on how to grow pumpkins, and how to write your name so that it grows into the pumpkin, as pictured in the book.

 ## Explore the Biology

As kids, we loved pumpkins not only for the holiday season they represented but also for their color and an outlandish size that appears in no other food available in a grocery store. When ripe, pumpkins play an important role in cultural events such as Halloween and Thanksgiving or harvest feasts, being used for jack-o-lanterns and pumpkin pie. Readers may be interested to learn that pumpkins were originally domesticated in North America. The gargantuan size that pumpkins can reach is a tribute to both genetics and optimal growing conditions, both of which are illustrated here. The focus of this book is this flowering plant's life cycle, but opportunities to delve more deeply into plant biology are abundant.

Each page provides major concepts that on their own could be the focus of an entire plant biology lesson, such as dicotyledonous (dicot) leaves, root architecture, trichomes (plant hairs), photosynthesis, leaf venation, floral attributes, pollination, senescence, and genetic diversity.

The poetic text will catalyze astute readers to search for the rich biological details contained in the detailed photographs. A clear example is on the page with five sprouting pumpkin seeds. The text reads "This garden will be home to many pumpkin cousins — the big pumpkin family, five varieties," and the image shows five seedlings that are morphologically distinct (differently shaped), illustrating genetic diversity within the pumpkin family. The following page reinforces this concept of heritable traits by showing that each of the seedlings originated from a seed that was structurally different from the others.

Pumpkin Life Cycle

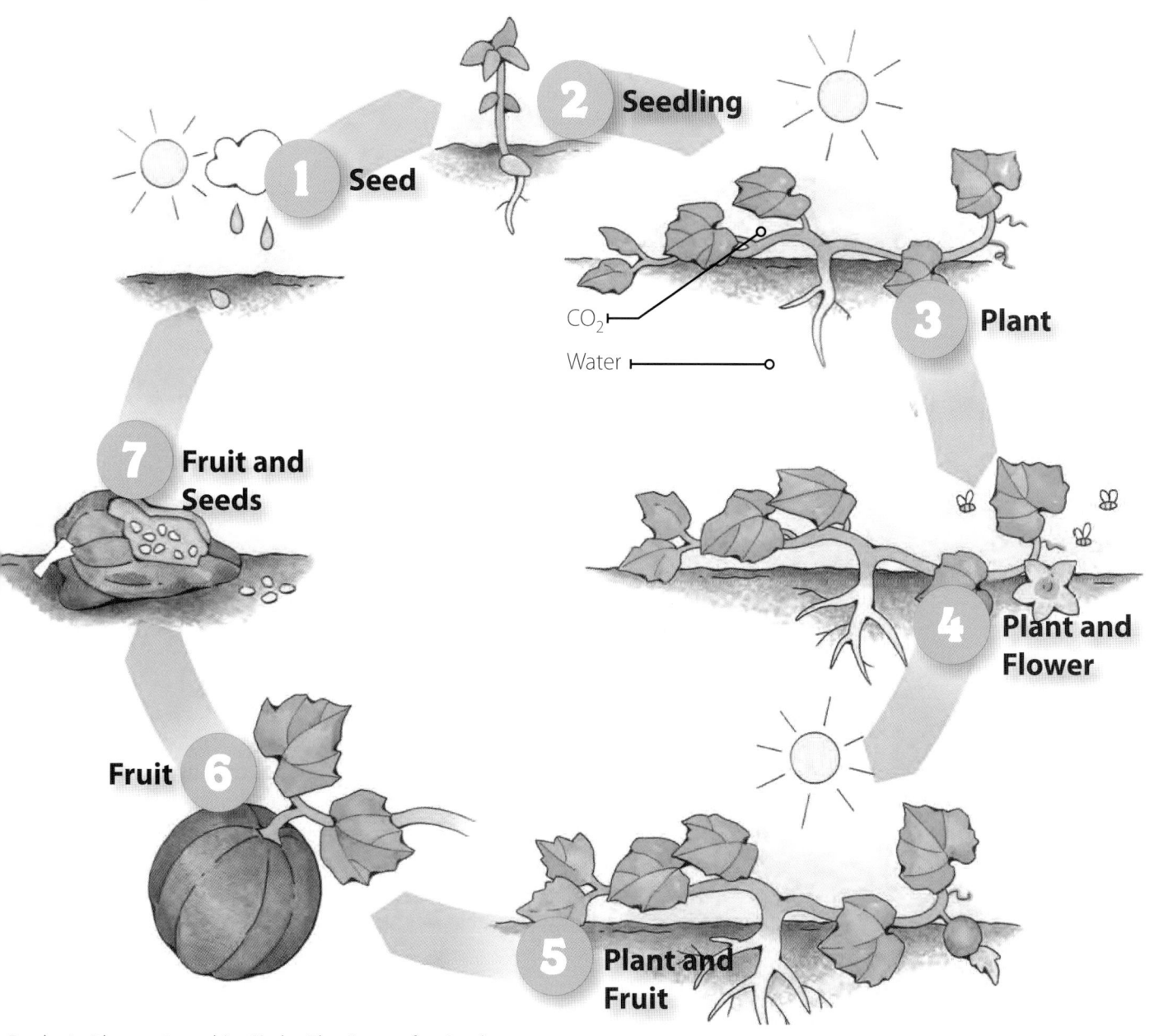

 **Digging Deeper**

Talking Points

1. How is a pumpkin like a circle?

Younger readers may immediately answer that a pumpkin is round, but the deeper metaphor of a circle reflects the seed-to-seed life cycle of a pumpkin. After reading the book, ask your readers to construct a life-cycle diagram for this plant. To help them become familiar with the stages, ask which stages they have the most experience with. Ask, "When do you usually see a pumpkin?" Challenge them to determine which stage comes immediately before and after the life stage they chose. Choose another familiar plant, like a dandelion, and describe its life cycle using the pumpkin life cycle as a comparison.

2. What does a pumpkin plant look like at each stage of its life cycle?

The authors use comparisons and metaphors to help readers understand the appearance of each stage of the cycle. Ask readers to identify phrases or words that helped them visualize the plant. Show a favorite page in the book and ask them to list alternative descriptors that they might use for the photos in this book or for other plants.

3. How did that pumpkin become so BIG?

Where does this mass come from? As shown in the book, pumpkin plants have a large leaf surface area (for example, see the page with orange gloved hands holding "huge green leaves..."). These natural solar collectors capture carbon dioxide through photosynthesis, convert it to a sugar, and send it to the growing pumpkin. This sugar, along with water, constitutes the new mass found in a growing pumpkin. Champion pumpkins can actually add more than 20 pounds a day of water and sugar weight!

Learning Experiences

1. Do pumpkin math.

Giant pumpkins can reach a weight of 1,000 pounds when they are harvested. Explain to the group that these fruits reach that size in about 100 days (although they do not gain much weight at the beginning or at the end). Ask your readers, "On average, how many pounds a day would a 900-pound pumpkin grow in a day or a week?"

People who grow giant pumpkins for competition will remove all but one or two pumpkins on a plant. Ask your readers why this is the case. Each plant can produce only so much mass in a growing season and consume only so much water. To maximize growth, gardeners limit the number of fruits while maximizing the water and photosynthetic output. Young gardeners may make connections here to thinning seedlings or fruits on other trees such as peaches or apples. Giant pumpkin plants can require more than 500 gallons of water per week and cover 600 to 700 square feet (picture one gallon of milk and measure a room for comparisons). If grown for 100 days, how much water would they require?

Related Texts

A Fruit Is a Suitcase for Seeds
(p.1)
Written by Jean Richards
Illustrated by Anca Hariton

Published by The Millbrook Press (2002)
Grade Level: K-2

• • • • • • • •

The Pumpkin Book
Written and Illustrated by Gail Gibbons

Published by Holiday House (1999)
Grade Level: K-3

• • • • • • • •

Pumpkin, Pumpkin
Written and Illustrated by Jeanne Titherington

Published by Greenwillow (1986)
Grade Level: K-2

A prize-winning pumpkin in our town weighed in at 888 pounds and stood as high as an adult's waist. Ask your readers how long it took the pumpkin to reach 888 pounds if it grew on average 8, 9, or 11 pounds per day.

2. Investigate pumpkin seeds.

The flesh of the pumpkin is used in many savory and sweet dishes, and the seeds can be toasted or used to make sauces. Get three strikingly different varieties of pumpkins (dwarf, baking, and carving) to see if the seeds differ in size. Carve the pumpkins, remove and wash the seeds, and then trace or make a rubbing of the seeds on paper. Be sure to keep track of each seed's origin. Measure or compare the size of the seeds (readers may want to calculate the average size) and compare them. As illustrated in the text, each variety is genetically distinct, which is manifested not only in fruit characteristics but also in other characteristics such as seed size. When you have finished measuring your seeds, toast them for a snack.

3. Create plant graffiti.

Writing your name in a surprising place has timeless appeal. If you grow pumpkin plants, invite your readers to try the name-engraving experience detailed in the back matter of the book. Let readers using a pen or knife to carve their names into the fruit. Supervise closely, making sure they cut just deep enough into the fruit to remove the outer layer of skin. As the fruit grows, so will the names. If pumpkins aren't available, this works with any type of squash; if many types are available, compare the outcomes.

Additional Resources

For more information about the pumpkin patch featured in this book, visit this website: *www.informeddemocracy.com/pumpkin/contents.html*

Just for fun: watch this video of a giant pumpkin regatta in Burlington, Vermont. *www.youtube.com/watch?v=QCqkHomnbHU*. If you are feeling adventurous, buy a miniature pumpkin, carve it into a boat and float it down your local creek.

 **Lesson Plan**

Pumpkin Seed Math

Objective	To practice estimating with pumpkin seeds.

Time	1 hour

Materials	• At least eight pumpkins of different sizes, shapes, and colors • Newspaper • Knife for adult • Large spoon • Bowls • Pumpkin Data Worksheets

Laying the Groundwork	Ask readers: • What part of the pumpkin plant is the fruit, and how do you know? (The pumpkin is the fruit because it contains seeds.) • How many seeds do you think each pumpkin contains? Do you think the number of seeds is the same for all the pumpkins? And if so, why or why not? (All pumpkins have different numbers of seeds. Some varieties have lots of seeds and others have only a few.

Exploration	1. Divide readers into four groups and give each group a pumpkin on which you have written a number.
	2. On their Pumpkin Data Worksheet, have readers write a description of their pumpkin's appearance, record the weight and circumference, and then estimate the number of seeds inside the pumpkin.
	3. Have an adult cut the top off each pumpkin and then let readers scoop out the seeds and count how many they find.
	4. Record the actual number of seeds and calculate the difference between the estimated and actual number of seeds.
	5. Give each group a second pumpkin and repeat the process. Compare the results to see whether there is any correlation between weight, circumference, and number of seeds. Ask your readers whether their ability to estimate improved the second time, and if so, why? You will probably find that there is no correlation between weight, circumference, and number of seeds, because the number of seeds is determined by fertilization (that is, the number of pollen grains that successfully fertilize the flower).

Branching Out Have readers compare the seeds from each of the pumpkins in appearance and size. Pumpkin seeds, also called pepitas, are green in color, often surrounded by an off-white seed coat Some varieties produce seeds without a shell. An energy-dense food, pumpkin seeds contain high levels of protein and fat along with important nutrients including vitamin E, tryptophan, zinc, iron, manganese, magnesium, phosphorus, and copper.

Toast the seeds and compare the taste. Preparing pumpkin seeds can be as easy as tossing the seeds in butter or oil, spreading them on a pan, sprinkling them with salt, then roasting in the oven for 45 minutes to an hour.

NAME   DATE

Pumpkin Data Worksheet

Pumpkin Number	Description	Weight	Circumference	Number of Seeds		
				Estimated (a)	Actual (b)	Difference (a - b)
1						
2						
3						
4						
5						
6						
7						
8						

Books In Bloom: Pumpkin Circle: The Story of a Garden

by Joyce Sidman
Illustrated by Beth Krommes

· · · · · · ·

Houghton Mifflin Harcourt (2011)
Grade Level: PreK-3

Swirl by Swirl: Spirals in Nature

 ## What We Love About This Book

- Luminous scratchboard illustrations
- Spirals found in unexpected places

 ## Discover the Book

This stunning book explores the occurrence of the spiral shape in nature. The Caldecott Award–winning team of author Joyce Sidman and artist Beth Krommes invites us to observe spirals found in flora and fauna, such as the proboscis of a Giant Swallowtail butterfly, a coiled bull snake, a tidal whirlpool, a spider's web, and a calla lily blossom. In simple yet descriptive language, Sidman lets us know that this spiral structure can offer strength, protection, warmth, and beauty. Strong, poetic words like clever, bold, and snuggling work surprisingly well to convey scientific phenomena such as hibernation, tornadoes, and plant development. Expanded explanations of the spiral's role in each of these are detailed in pages at the back of the book.

Krommes's signature illustrations — watercolor painted over black and white scratchboard — produce lustrous scenes of spirals in the ocean, sky, and woods. The black lines and rich colors create landscapes that are simultaneously gorgeous and accurate; small textual labels identify the types of plant, animal, or weather featured on each page.

 ## Explore the Biology

Patterns abound in nature, whether in clouds, leaves, seasons, or birdsongs. Patterns are inherently intriguing, but one complex pattern, the spiral, is especially compelling. As plant biologists, we like to quote the explanation of "mathemusician" Vi Hart: "This pattern is not just useful, not just beautiful, it's inevitable...." This book explores spirals found in nature ranging from well-known examples such as the sunflower and tornado to less-obvious ones such as a developing fern frond. In the biological world, spirals serve many functions. Spirals are an efficient way to package a large item into a small space. Imagine a butterfly flying with its proboscis unrolled — the proboscis would be unwieldy, suffer damage, and cause erratic flight. Spirals also play a role in defense, protection, and heat conservation. In this book, these concepts are conveyed through illustrations of a Merino sheep's horn, a snail's shell, and a curled snake.

The Fibonacci sequence (defined in the Learning Experiences) is also introduced, as shown by the sunflower, rose, daisy, and aloe plant. For centuries, mathematicians and biologists have pondered why the leaves on a stem or petals on a flower are arranged in this mathematical pattern. Both single and double spirals can be found in the illustrations. Single spirals are just that — one continuous line, as in the fern frond. Double spirals, such as the sunflower, have one spiral oriented in a clockwise direction and one oriented counterclockwise. Why do plants produce their petals and leaves in this pattern? Originally it was thought that leaf and petal spirals minimized competition between leaves and maximized seed packing. Today we know that petal and leaf arrangements are really caused by early developmental events related to hormones and most likely did not evolve to increase leaf, petal, or seed packing.

Digging Deeper

Talking Points

1. Why is it so easy to identify the spirals in these busy illustrations?

   Ask your readers how the artist calls our attention to the spirals in each tail, plant, and wave. Krommes relies on deep black lines, and sometimes white space, to highlight each spiral.

2. What is a spiral? Are there different types of spirals?

   After reading the text, ask your readers to come up with a working definition of a spiral. Ask them if there are different types of spirals, using the images in the text to help them answer. A spiral is defined as a curved lined moving away from or toward a common origin. Spirals can be continuous, as with a line that winds its way from the center, as seen in the snail shell, spiderweb, or curled-up snake. They can also be made of many lines or arms that emanate from a common point, as with the Milky Way or the center of a sunflower.

3. What do spirals do in nature?

   The star of this book is the spiral. In addition to being visually interesting, what functions does the spiral play in biology? Using the text, invite your readers to notice how this shape plays a role in protection (snail), defense (sheep's horn), and packaging (proboscis). Ask your readers to find other examples of how spirals facilitate these functions.

Related Texts

The Reason for a Flower
Written and Illustrated by
Ruth Heller

Published by Puffin Press (1999)
Grade Level: PreK-3

Learning Experiences

1. **Explore the Fibonacci sequence.**

   Mathematically, many spirals can be described by a numerical pattern called the Fibonacci sequence. The Fibonacci sequence describes a series of numbers in which each number is the sum of the two that preceded it. The sequence 0, 1, 1, 2, 3, 5, 8, 13, 21 is produced from the following equations:

   a. $0+1=1$

   b. $1+1=2$

   c. $1+2=3$

   d. $2+3=5$

   e. $3+5=8$

   f. $5+8=13$

   g. $8+13=21$

2. **Scratch away!**

   Imitate Krommes's technique by making or obtaining scratchboard — white paper (or even fine white clay) covered with a layer of black India ink. As an image is scratched into the surface, the white is revealed and the illustration becomes lighter. At this point in the technique, Krommes makes several photocopies of these etchings and tries out different watercolors on these copies. Copy your readers' scratched images so that they too can experiment with different watercolor versions of their etchings. Once they have experience with this technique, challenge your artists to illustrate the concept of spirals, or even a plant with the Fibonacci sequence.

3. **Spirals in biology.**

   Have your readers draw a plant or animal using a spiral template. Ask them if the spiral structure helps that organism with protection, packaging, or warmth. Categorize their drawings when everyone has finished.

 **Lesson Plan**

Sequence of Spirals

Objective	To explore the Fibonacci sequence.
Time	1 hour
Materials	• Sunflower image • Colored pencils
Laying the Groundwork	Ask readers: • **What is a numerical sequence?** (It is a series of numbers listed in a specific order.)

Exploration	1. **Mathematically, many spirals can be described by a numerical pattern called the Fibonacci sequence.** The Fibonacci sequence describes a series of numbers in which each number is the sum of the two that preceded it. The sequence 0, 1, 1, 2, 3, 5, 8, 13, 21 is produced from the following equations: a. $0+1=1$ b. $1+1=2$ c. $1+2=3$ d. $2+3=5$ e. $3+5=8$ f. $5+8=13$ g. $8+13=21$ 2. **Using the image of the sunflower and colored pencils, ask your readers to trace the spiral arms in the flower.** They should identify two sets of arms, one that goes clockwise and one that goes counterclockwise. Color each set a different color. 3. **Have readers count the number of arms in each spiral.** These two numbers should be two Fibonacci sequence numbers, 8 and 13.
Branching Out	Take a nature walk or visit a garden to see if readers can find examples of spirals. Things you may find include pinecones, asters, and leaves on a stem.

NAME   DATE

Sunflower Spiral

TELL ME, TREE

All about Trees for Kids

by Gail Gibbons

Written and Illustrated by Gail Gibbons

· · · · · · ·

Published by Little Brown & Co. (2002)
Grade Level: 1-4

Tell Me, Tree: All about Trees for Kids

 ## What We Love About This Book

- Pleasing and accurate watercolor illustrations
- A complete children's guide to tree biology
- Strong examples of nonfiction features

 ## Discover the Book

This book offers a wealth of information about generic tree structures and growth, the role trees play in the ecosystem, and specific strategies for identifying trees. Gail Gibbons has so much to say about trees that her text and illustrations spill over onto the copyright page, and the concepts, vocabulary, and processes described could constitute an entire teaching unit. A brief environmental message about thoughtful stewardship in the growing and harvesting of trees is included toward the end of the book. Back matter includes suggestions and directions for tree-related activities that will have junior arborists eager to press leaves and make bark rubbings to create their own tree identification book.

Framed by the arboreal green end pages, Gibbons's skillful watercolor illustrations are accurate in their color, scale, detail, and texture. Her deliberate use of cross-sections, arrows, diagrams, labels, and sequence boxes not only informs readers about trees, but provides a strong model of how to convey information effectively. This appealing work of nonfiction is an excellent model for reports that are commonly written in elementary classrooms. Those familiar with Gibbons's high-quality books can be assured that this is one of her best.

 ## Explore the Biology

Tell Me, Tree contains an impressive amount of tree biology that helps to answer two questions: what is a tree, and what separates one type of tree from another? Gibbons explores the first of these themes by deftly leading the reader through the defining characteristics of a tree. Her explanations are remarkably comprehensive, and topics such as tree structure, organs, physiology, life cycle, and growth requirements are all addressed through complementary text and illustrations. For example, on a page with a crabapple branch, she writes, "Trees use food from their leaves to grow new wood, branches, twigs, buds, leaves, seeds, nuts, and fruit. The fruit of trees is often sweet from the sugar the leaves make. Trees need their food to stay alive and renew their growth." This short yet clear paragraph accurately captures how the process of photosynthesis in leaves produces sugars that are the building blocks and energy source for the rest of the plant.

Embedded within Gibbons's tour of tree biology is the concept that tree species have distinct differences despite their commonalities. For example, on a page focusing on seeds, Gibbons writes, "all trees, even the biggest, begin their lives as seeds. These seeds come in different shapes and sizes." Accompanying illustrations depict 14 dramatically different seed types. In a thorough cross-species comparison, Gibbons explores differences in leaves, fruit, stature, bark, shape, height, and environment.

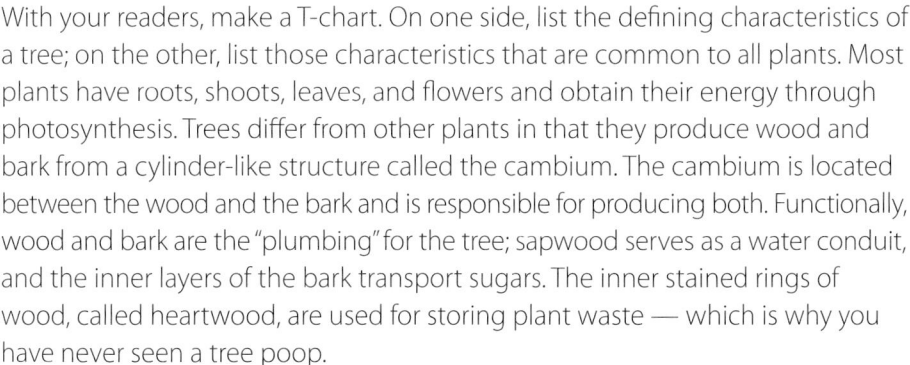 Digging Deeper

Talking Points

1. What is a tree?

   With your readers, make a T-chart. On one side, list the defining characteristics of a tree; on the other, list those characteristics that are common to all plants. Most plants have roots, shoots, leaves, and flowers and obtain their energy through photosynthesis. Trees differ from other plants in that they produce wood and bark from a cylinder-like structure called the cambium. The cambium is located between the wood and the bark and is responsible for producing both. Functionally, wood and bark are the "plumbing" for the tree; sapwood serves as a water conduit, and the inner layers of the bark transport sugars. The inner stained rings of wood, called heartwood, are used for storing plant waste — which is why you have never seen a tree poop.

2. How do you recognize a tree?

   With your readers, use the pages at the end of the book to explore the question: *how do we distinguish between trees?* Sixteen different tree species are shown that are distinguishable by five characteristics: leaf shape, leaf arrangement, tree shape (architecture), bark texture, and bark color. Have your readers generate a list of descriptors for each of these. For example, leaves could be described as having smooth or rough edges or being lobed or not lobed. After creating a beginning list of descriptors, play an identification game using the images on these pages. Hold the book so all can see and ask a reader to describe the characteristics of one tree while others try to guess its identity. Add words to your list that have been particularly helpful at identifying the trees.

3. Why do plants need light?

   Many trees weigh thousands of pounds, and what is remarkable is that the vast majority of this mass came from the gas carbon dioxide, which was incorporated through a process called photosynthesis. Using the page titled "Leaves," ask your readers, "Since trees do not eat, what do they need to grow?" Readers will most likely respond that plants get their energy from sunlight. Build on this idea by asking, "How do they use sunlight?" During photosynthesis, light energy is used to build plant molecules out of carbon dioxide. What is mind-boggling is that virtually every carbon atom in a tree came from a gas! Plants also need water, an integral component in the growth process.

Related Texts

Leaf Man

Written and Illustrated by
Lois Ehlert

Published by Harcourt Books (2005)
Grade Level: K-2

Learning Experiences

1. **Match the leaf.**

   Gather a variety of leaves and make rubbings by placing leaves under a piece of white paper and gently coloring over them with crayons. Display the leaf rubbings on a wall, distribute the real leaves, and challenge your readers to match each leaf to a rubbing. Ask readers what characteristics of their leaf enabled them to make a match. Encourage such descriptors of the leaves as "needle/broadleaf" and "lobed/not lobed"; consider size and texture. A similar activity with bark rubbings would reinforce the idea that although trees share characteristics, they also have differences. (Avoid peeling the bark from trees, as that may damage the cambium and kill the tree.)

2. **Create a tree identification book.**

   Given the large number of trees, start with the most common ones in your area so that your readers can learn to identify those that are most prevalent in their surroundings. An easy way to start would be with your leaf or bark rubbings. Photos and sketches could also be used.

3. **Take a look inside a tree.**

   Using the tree cross-section reproducible or a piece of firewood, have your readers identify the sapwood, heartwood, annual rings, and bark. Have them count the number of annual rings to determine the age of the tree, keeping in mind that the width of each ring is a reflection of the growing conditions that year.

Comparison of Cross-Section of a Tree and Non-Woody Plant

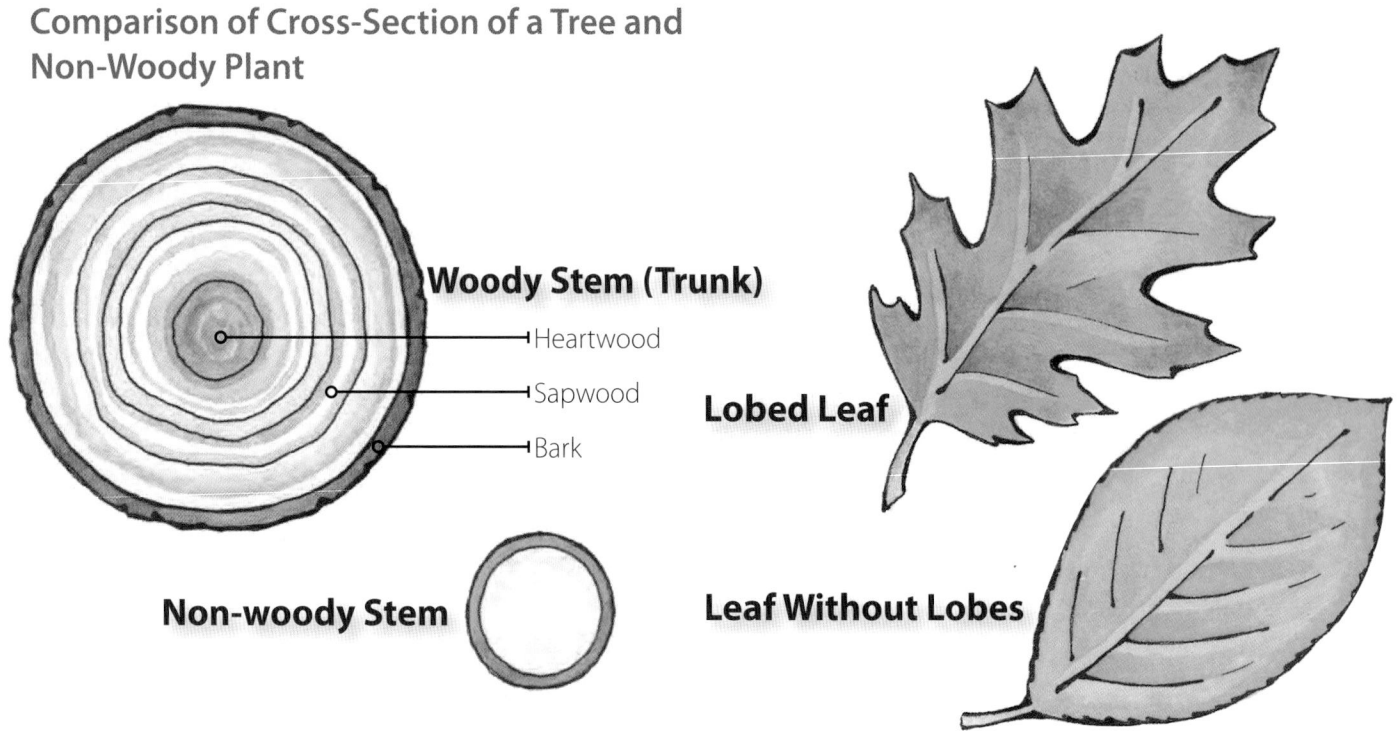

Woody Stem (Trunk)

Heartwood

Sapwood

Bark

Non-woody Stem

Lobed Leaf

Leaf Without Lobes

Books In Bloom: Tell Me, Tree: All about Trees for Kids

**Lesson Plan**

Inside a Tree

Objective   To explore the basic structure of trees.

Time   1 hour

Materials
- Tree cross-section figure
- Optional: pieces of trunk or branches cut so you can see the inner rings of the tree
- Cross-section of a non-woody plant

Laying the Groundwork   Ask readers:
- **What is a tree, and how are trees different from other plants?**
  (Just like most other plants, trees have roots, shoots, leaves, and flowers [or pinecones], and obtain their energy through photosynthesis. Trees differ from other plants in that they produce wood and bark from a cylinder-like structure called the cambium. The cambium is located between the wood and bark and is responsible for producing both. Functionally, wood and bark are the "plumbing" for the tree; sapwood serves as a water conduit and the inner layers of the bark transport sugars. The inner stained rings of wood, called heartwood, are used for storing plant waste — which is why you have never seen a tree poop.)

Exploration
1. **Take a look inside a tree.**
   Using the tree cross-section figure or a piece of wood cut from a branch or trunk (such as firewood), have your readers identify the sapwood, heartwood, annual rings, and bark.

2. **Compare the cross-section of a tree to the cross-section of a non-woody plant.**
   Ask readers to describe differences and discuss how the insides of the plants and trees affect their ultimate mature size and shape. (See illustration on page 95.)

Branching Out   Have readers count the number of annual rings to determine the age of the tree, keeping in mind that the width of each ring is a reflection of the growing conditions that year. Years that were particularly wet will have produced larger rings than dry years because the tree produced more wood those years.

Ask your readers to identify the wetter years and then check their assessments by visiting *www.noaa.gov* for historical rainfall data. If the tree is decades old, you may want to spend some time making connections between each ring and local or national historical events.

NAME

DATE

Tree Cross Section

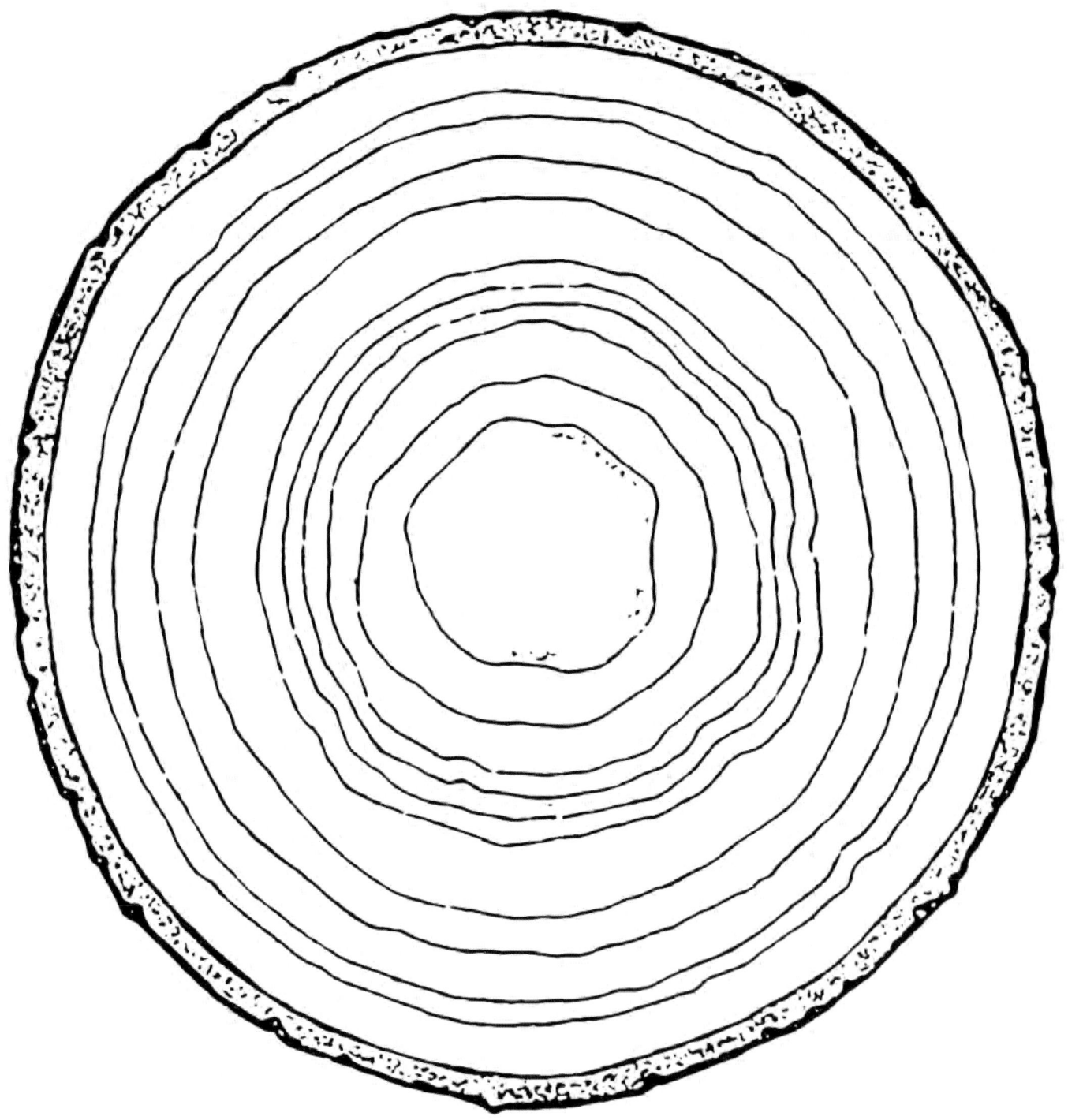

by Sarah Stewart
Illustrated by David Small

. . . .

Farrar, Straus, and Giroux (1997)
Grade Level: 1-3

The Gardener

 What We Love About This Book

- Embedded story of the cat
- Rooftop gardening
- Plucky self-determination

 Discover the Book

Set during the Great Depression, this Caldecott Honor book tells the story of a girl who is sent to live with her baker uncle in the city as her family back home copes with job losses and hunger. Lydia Grace Finch's letters to her parents and grandmother tell the story of her trip, her adjustment to life in a dreary city, and her plucky determination to bring flowers to her new home and a smile to her uncle's face. Lydia Grace spends almost a year with Uncle Jim; signs of passing time include the dates on Lydia Grace's letters, a Christmas tree, and Fourth of July sparklers. The structure of the calendar year allows the reader to gain a sense of the life cycle of bulb planting and blooming.

In the same way that many of us seek solace and pleasure in our gardens, Lydia Grace turns to gardening to cope with the difficulties of her situation. Her gardens are an extension of her family's traditions, and reflect personal characteristics such as determination and optimism, as well as showcasing her horticultural know-how. There are plenty of details to pore over in the award-winning illustrations. Attentive readers of all ages will enjoy the historical details of the buildings and the workings of the bakery as well as the delightfully embedded story of the cat. David Small uses pen and ink to convey facial expressions that show character development, and watercolors to present both the monochromatic dreariness of the Great Depression and the bright-colored flowers that sustain Lydia Grace and offer the ultimate surprise that makes Uncle Jim smile.

 Explore the Biology

Lydia Grace is a child who endures extraordinary hardships with poise, and from the beginning it is clear that she is a gardener. This is actually the central botanical theme explored in this book — what is a gardener? In the opening end page, Lydia Grace is seen in a flourishing garden back home with her grandmother. The size and scope of this space establishes that this is a family that knows how to garden. In contrast, Lydia Grace arrives in the city in summer — which should be the peak of the growing season — yet not a single plant is seen and, equally surprising, no soil is evident. Without these two key elements (plants and soil), is it possible to still be a gardener? Undeterred, Lydia Grace assembles what she needs: seeds, bulbs, and soil, but the key challenge for an urban gardener is space, which Lydia Grace eventually finds in "cracked teacups and bent cake pans."

Digging Deeper

Talking Points

1. Why does Lydia Grace garden?

   Lydia Grace must move to the city while her family experiences hardship on the farm. Of all the ways that she might have remembered her family, ask your readers to explore why she chooses to create a garden.

2. How does Lydia Grace start a garden?

   Lydia Grace finds herself in an environment very different from the farm. She must find a way to start a garden while living in an apartment building rather than an open landscape. Ask your readers what the differences are between a farm and an urban landscape. What are the challenges of gardening in the latter, and how did she overcome them?

3. What is a garden?

   Use the illustrations on the front end pages as an example of a garden. Ask your readers to compare these pictures to Lydia Grace's plantings seen in her window boxes, her shelves, and the rooftop garden. Do they consider container plantings to be "gardens"? Why or why not? This question is open-ended, but help your readers consider the differences and similarities between the rooftop garden, which is composed entirely of planted containers, and the single container shown on the page with the April 27 letter. This comparison invites readers to consider how they would define a garden. Can they describe other types of gardens they have seen? Although most gardens include plants and soil, they differ greatly in terms of types of plants and physical space. Keep an ongoing list of the types of gardens your readers encounter in literature and in their lives throughout the year.

Related Books

Wanda's Roses (p.112)
Written by Pat Brisson
Illustrated by Maryann
Cocca-Leffler

Published by Boyds Mills Press (1994)
Grade Level: K-2

• • • • • • • •

**Stringbean's Trip to the
Shining Sea** (a tale told in
epistolary form)
Written and Illustrated by Vera B.
Williams and Jennifer Williams

*Published by Greenwillow
Books (1988)*
Grade Level: PreK-2

• • • • • • • •

Flower Garden
Written by Eve Bunting
Illustrated by Kathryn Hewitt

*Published by Red Wagon Books/
Harcourt (2008)*
Grade Level: PreK-2

Learning Experiences

1. Experiment with container gardens.

Demonstrate how container size affects plant growth by planting your own container gardens. Begin by asking your readers to predict how soil volume affects root growth. Test their hypothesis by planting the same plants in a variety of containers, such as a yogurt container, a milk jug, and a bucket. If possible, also plant one in the ground for another comparison. It may be helpful to begin the discussion by asking how the yogurt container, milk jug, bucket, and in-ground gardens differ. Your readers will probably notice that the growing space changes dramatically as you move from a small yogurt container to a milk jug and then to the infinite outdoors. Because they are small, containers limit root growth, which can affect the plant size. Conversely, unlimited space typically allows for more extensive root growth, and plants can grow larger, as shown by the sunflower towering over Lydia Grace's grandmother in the front end pages. Collect data and compare the results.

2. You be the roots!

In a large, open space, place hula hoops on the floor. Tell readers that each hoop represents a planting container, and ask each of them to first curl up inside a hoop and to then spread their limbs (representing plant roots) to the limits of the hoop. Ask them to do the same spreading exercise on the floor without any limits. What connections can they make to plants?

3. Write an epistolary story.

Lydia Grace's story takes place when cellphones and personal computers didn't exist and telephones were expensive to use. The author chose to tell the story through Lydia Grace's letters to her family; that is, the book is an epistolary story. Invite your readers to write their own story through a series of letters.

101

 **Lesson Plan**

Comparing Containers

Objective	To demonstrate the effect of container size on plant growth.

Time	8 or more weeks

Materials
- Six to 10 seeds or plants of the same variety
- An assortment of containers representing various sizes, from small (yogurt container) to large (5-gallon bucket)
- Potting soil
- Plant Growth Table (see below)
- Ruler

Laying the Groundwork

Ask readers:
- **Why do plants have roots?**
  (Roots provide water and nutrients, and help anchor the plants in the ground.)

- **How big are plant roots?**
  (The size varies greatly from plant to plant. Some plants have lots of roots of equal size, called fibrous roots. Other plants have one main root, called a taproot, with lots of smaller roots shooting off the sides.)

- **How does growing the plant in a container affect its roots?**
  How might the size of the container be important? How might the health and size of plant roots affect the health and size of the plant above the ground? (Containers limit root growth, which can affect the plant size.)

Exploration

1. Obtain six to 10 plants of the same variety.
   Try to find plants that are of approximately equal size. Alternatively, if time allows, you can start plants from seed.

2. Collect an assortment of containers in various sizes.
   You can use traditional containers such as clay or plastic pots, or creative containers such as yogurt cups, milk jugs, or plastic buckets. Just make sure all containers have drainage holes at the bottom. You can add holes with a small drill if necessary.

3. Using one type of potting soil mix in all containers (to control the variables), plant your seeds or seedlings in the containers and then water.

   Measure the volume of potting soil mix added to each container and record it on the Plant Growth Table. As a group, predict which container will produce the healthiest and largest plant.

4. Place the containers in the same location to make sure all receive the same light and experience the same temperatures.

   Measure growth weekly by recording height. Depending on the type of plant, you can also measure growth by recording leaf count. If possible, take digital pictures of the plants for later comparison.

5. After the last measurement, remove the plants from the containers and very carefully brush away the soil.

   Take digital photos of each sample for comparison (keep the container in the background of the photo, or label each photo to make sure the samples are not confused). If your plants have taproots, measure the length. If your plants have fibrous roots, compare growth by counting the number of roots, weighing the roots, or simply ranking them from smallest to largest by sight.

6. Compile all results and discuss.

   Did the container size affect the root growth? Did the container size affect the above ground growth? Did your prediction for the healthiest and largest plant hold true? What did you learn about selecting containers for planting?

Branching Out

Explore container gardens further by designing experiments to compare different types of growing media (such as commercial potting soil mixes, garden soil, compost, sand, and peat moss) and different varieties of plants. You can also alter light conditions, watering patterns, and types and amounts of fertilizer.

NAME _____

DATE _____

Plant Growth Table

Plant Number	Type of Container	Volume of Soil	Height								Root Growth
			Week 1	Week 2	Week 3	Week 4	Week 5	Week 6	Week 7	Week 8	
1											
2											
3											
4											
5											
6											
7											
8											
9											
10											

![The Wind's Garden book cover](title image)

by Bethany Roberts • illustrated by Melanie Hope Greenberg

by Bethany Roberts
Illustrated by Melanie Hope Greenberg

Published by Henry Holt (2001)
Grade Level: K-2

The Wind's Garden

 ## What We Love About This Book

• Bright illustrations and introduction to seed dispersal for young readers

 ## Discover the Book

In this comparative tale, a girl plants a garden and the wind plants one, too. In simple, first-person narrative, the girl describes the development of the two gardens through a growing season, including their need for water, sun, and soil. The structure of the book illuminates the similarities and differences between the two gardens. The text and illustrations work together as the font size grows along with the flowers.

Greenberg's cheerful illustrations present the differences in the two gardens. The color choices are bright and believable, beginning with spring green and deepening through the lush growing season of summer. Close-ups and bird's-eye views invite readers to gauge the size, shape, and progress of each garden as the flowers mature.

The author's note includes suggestions for growing one's own garden with flowers that are quick to germinate. Tips are also included for observing "the wind's garden." Young children will quickly grasp the comparison between natural seed dispersal and cultivation; older readers may gain an appreciation for the wildflowers they observe in their daily lives.

 ## Explore the Biology

From a biological perspective, this is a rich text with two central themes. The first is that the plants in the girl's garden have the same needs as the plants in the wind's garden; regardless of which garden they are in, plants require water, space, and light to grow. A second and more pronounced theme is the comparison between a garden and nature. Stylized illustrations coupled with carefully chosen text illustrate the key points. For example, the girl's garden is planted in an orderly fashion, as opposed to the wind's garden, which is randomly colonized by seeds dispersed by the wind through their dry and wispy fruits. As the book progresses, the contrast between the two gardens becomes more obvious: the wind's garden displays increased species diversity, larger biomass, and an apparent lack of order. Whereas both gardens are presented as aesthetically pleasing, the wind's garden is presented as richer in color, animals, and insects. This is, of course, true to science; most cultivated gardens require energy inputs in the forms of labor, irrigation, and fertilizers, and yet meadows are often more species-diverse and biologically productive.

Digging Deeper

Talking Points

1. **What do all plants need to grow?**
   Ask your readers to find clues in the text and illustrations about what nature provides and what the girl provides. Possible responses include water, sun, soil, seed dispersal — through the wind or even the little girl — and pollinators such as bees and butterflies.

2. **How do the two gardens compare in terms of color, plant variety, organization, pollinators, and plant size?**
   Work with the book to deepen the readers' understanding by examining pages that offer striking comparisons between the two gardens. For example, the two pages illustrating the words "and GREW" show that the plants in the wind's garden are bigger, more varied, and more numerous, and are inhabited by birds, animals, and insects.

3. **How do seeds travel?**
   In this book, the plants are using the wind and their dried fruits to disperse their seeds and propagate. For example, the dandelion seed, familiar to many, is carried by a light parachute-like fruit that enables it to travel on the wind. Reexamine the page where this phenomenon is artistically represented with white spirals. Begin a discussion regarding whether or not all seeds can travel on the wind. Consider which physical characteristics make travel possible for some seeds and impossible for others.

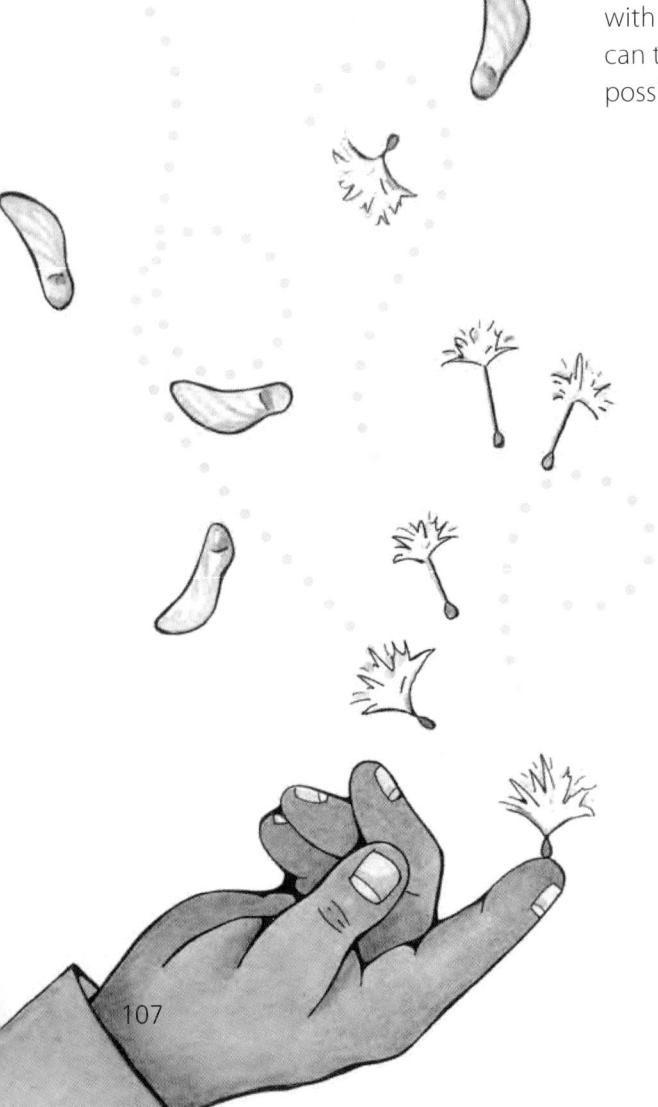

Learning Experiences

1. Compare the two gardens.

Have your readers make a T-chart showing the differences and commonalities between the two gardens.

Sample T-Chart

Wind's Garden	Girl's Garden
The wind plants seeds	The girl plants seeds
Sun provides light	Sun provides light
Watered by rain only	Girl waters with watering can
Not weeded	Weeded
Pollinators (bees, butterflies)	Pollinators (bees, butterflies)
High diversity	Low diversity
Randomly planted	Orderly
Larger plants	Smaller plants

2. Re-create the gardens.

Using the T-chart, young readers could act out or make a model of the two gardens to deepen their understanding. Children could role-play the flowers, pollinators, rain, animals, wind, and girl. Alternatively, they could use craft materials to create small models of these elements and place them in the "wind's garden" or the "girl's garden."

3. Search for wind-dispersed seeds.

What plants use the wind? Explore your outdoor surroundings with your readers and identify plants that use the wind to disperse their seeds. Some common plants that fall into this category: maples, dandelions, cottonwoods, and milkweed. Emphasize that if the seed is attached to a gossamer-like structure or floats like a helicopter, it is probably carried by the wind.

Related Texts

A Fruit Is a Suitcase for Seeds (p.1)
Written by Jean Richards
Illustrated by Anca Hariton

Published by The Millbrook Press (2002)
Grade Level: K-2

. . . .

Dandelions: Stars in the Grass
Written and Illustrated by Mia Posada

Published by Carolrhoda Books (2000)
Grade Level: K-5

. . . .

Flip, Float, Fly: Seeds on the Move
Written by JoAnn Macken
Illustrated by Pamela Popparone

Published by Holiday House (2008)
Grade Level: K-4

 **Lesson Plan**

Flying Seeds

Objective	To explore fruit characteristics that enable wind dispersal.
Time	1 hour
Materials	• Examples of fruits that enable seeds to be dispersed by the wind, such as fruit from maples, dandelions, cottonwoods, and milkweed • Examples of fruits not dispersed by the wind, such as coconuts, peaches, or watermelons • An assortment of craft supplies
Laying the Groundwork	Ask readers: • **Why do seeds travel?** (To colonize a new niche and to move away from the parent or sibling plants to avoid competition for resources like nutrients, sunlight, and water.) • **What kind of characteristics do you think seeds carried by the wind would possess?** (They are lightweight and attached to a structure evolved to help them float in the air.)

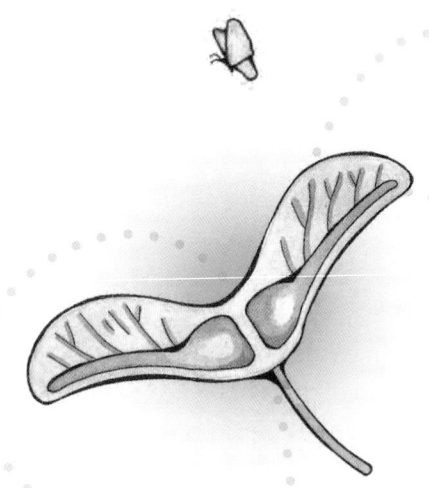

Exploration

1. **Give readers a chance to explore the examples of fruits and seeds you collected.**

   Observe the fruits and seeds, and on the basis of their visual appearance alone, hypothesize which are dispersed by the wind and which are not. Have your readers explain their reasoning.

2. **Test the predictions by dropping the fruits to the ground to see which float in the wind (do not do this with a watermelon unless you are prepared to clean up the mess!).**

   Ask readers to list the common characteristics of those seeds dispersed by the wind.

3. **Take the readers outside and identify plants with fruits developing on them.**

   Ask them to predict, using the knowledge they gained from the seed-drop experience, how these seeds might travel.

4. **Return inside and ask readers to design their own seed that would disperse using the wind.**

   Provide time for them to share their creation with others.

Branching Out Explore another mode of seed dispersal. Many seeds are designed to attach to clothing or animal fur to hitch a ride to a new location. Travel to a natural meadow area and put a pair of large socks over your shoes and/or your readers' shoes. Walk through the meadow, then remove the socks. Back inside, examine them with a hand lens and look for seeds. You can even plant the seeds in a container of soil and see what happens.

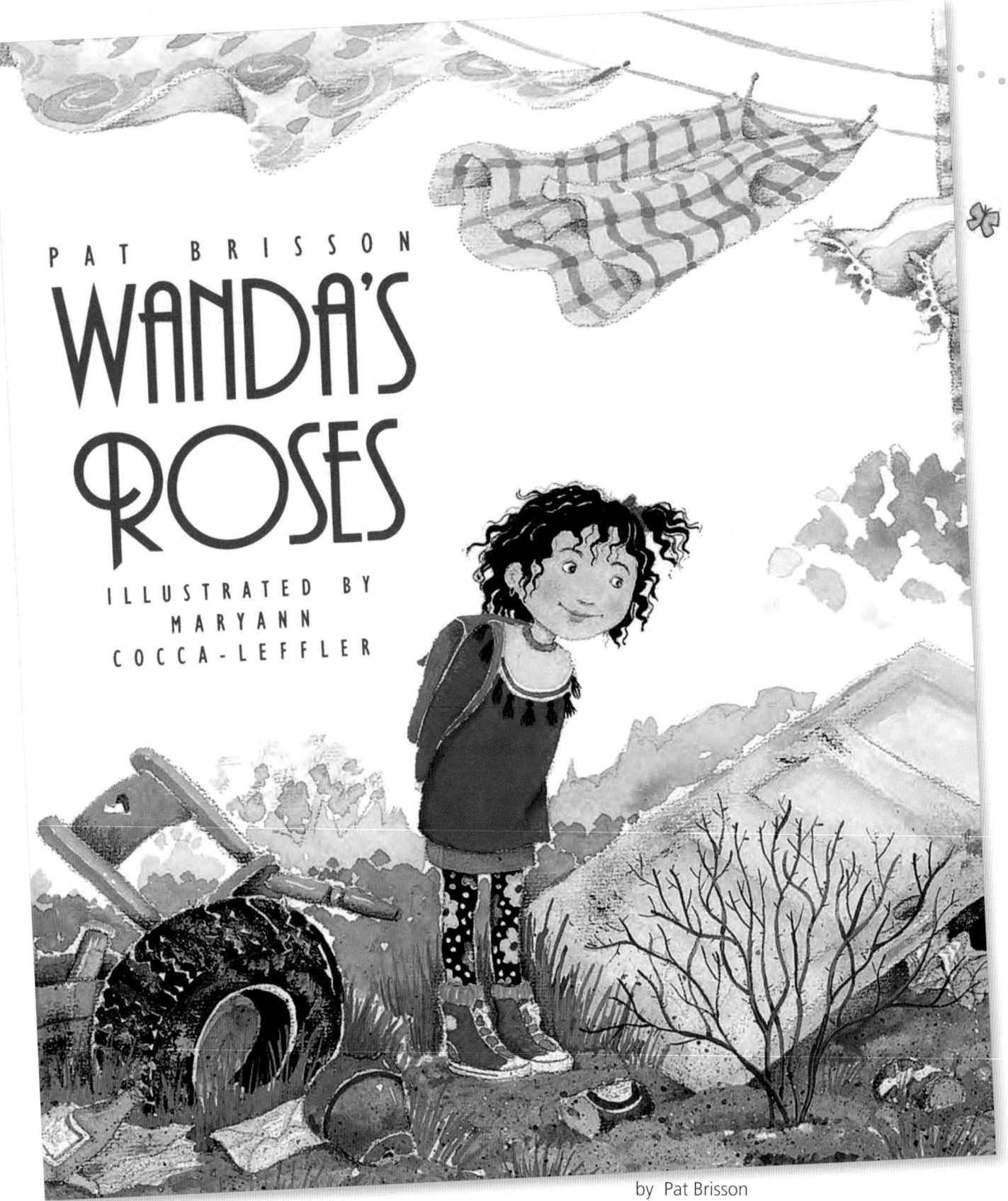

PAT BRISSON

WANDA'S ROSES

ILLUSTRATED BY
MARYANN
COCCA-LEFFLER

by Pat Brisson
Illustrated by Maryann Cocca-Leffler

· · · · · · ·

Published by Boyds Mills Press (1994)
Grade Level: K-2

Wanda's Roses

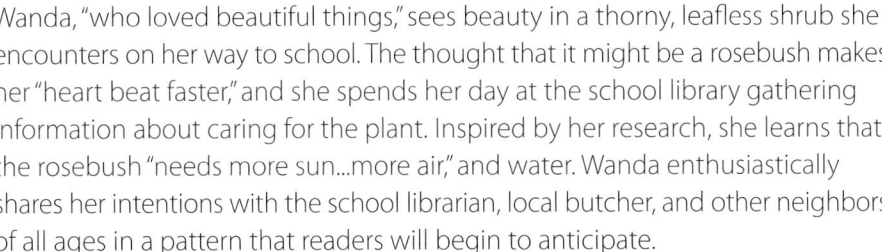

 ## What We Love About This Book

- Civic engagement of neighborhood
- Wanda's optimism
- The importance of plant identification

 ## Discover the book

Wanda, "who loved beautiful things," sees beauty in a thorny, leafless shrub she encounters on her way to school. The thought that it might be a rosebush makes her "heart beat faster," and she spends her day at the school library gathering information about caring for the plant. Inspired by her research, she learns that the rosebush "needs more sun...more air," and water. Wanda enthusiastically shares her intentions with the school librarian, local butcher, and other neighbors of all ages in a pattern that readers will begin to anticipate.

Although each of the neighbors may privately express skepticism, for example, "If that's a rosebush, then I'll be the King of France," they gamely support Wanda by joining her in cleaning litter from the vacant lot and offering advice, books, and buckets of water. When the neighborhood is invited to a Saturday morning tea, Wanda and her guests have surprises in store for each other. As the garden blossoms in an unusual way, the neighborhood agrees that the roses are indeed finally fit for a king or queen. Sharp-eyed readers will notice the rose motif on Wanda's hat and vest, on Mrs. Gamoni's dress, and of course, on the invitations to tea. The gentle gouache and colored pencil illustrations portray a tale of contagious optimism and civic engagement.

 ## Explore the Biology

From a biological perspective, this book explores how we recognize plants; more specifically, what distinguishes a rosebush from other plants? Wanda knows from previous experience that roses have thorns and that they grow as a bush, and she uses these two criteria to misidentify the plant. The adults in the story recognize the plant as something other than a rosebush, although it is never revealed how. Misidentification is a common occurrence because many plants share characteristics such as leaf shape, stature, and thorniness, but each species also has a defining set of characteristics that distinguish it. Understanding that organisms have unique features is an important biological concept because these differences reflect evolutionary history and are quite literally what separates one species from its relatives. Plant identification is important to gardeners because if they don't know what they are growing, they can't meet that plant's needs (and they will be crummy weeders). Scientists use a range of tools to identify plants, such as dichotomous keys that can be used by everyone, or even highly specialized tools such as DNA analysis.

 **Digging Deeper**

Talking Points

1. **How did Wanda learn what her plant needed to grow?**

   What did she learn about her plant's needs? Wanda uses direct observation, art, specialized books, and experts to gather information. Through the course of the book, Wanda clears away trash for air circulation and sun, waters the shrub, and gives her plant time to grow.

2. **How did Wanda get her neighbors involved in her project?**

   Ask your readers to describe how Wanda got her neighbors involved in her project. Wanda's efforts demonstrate the essence of a "think globally, act locally" approach, and her dedication and focus make this a successful project.

3. **Why is beauty important?**

   In this text, Wanda nurtures a "rosebush" to beautify her neighborhood. Begin by asking your readers what they find beautiful in their surrounding — such as their room, a playground, or a park — and then ask them to describe why. Help younger readers by having them identify shape, texture, color, size, or scent. Next, explore why we value beauty in our environment. Help your readers discover that we do not all find the same things beautiful. Wanda finds plants beautiful. Ask your readers if plants and flowers appeal to them, and if so, why.

Learning Experiences

1. **Make a dichotomous key.**

   Start with something simple like fruits, writing implements, or friends, and list binary attributes using a "yes/no" or "either/or" format (see Lesson Plan).

2. **Create your own beautification art project.**

   Have your readers pick an area of their home, school, neighborhood, or town that they would like to beautify. Invite them to draw or paint this area on paper and then add the elements that they would use to beautify this space.

3. **Pick a community service project.**

   Wanda is a catalyst for a community project as she follows her own interest in the rosebush. Encourage your readers to look locally and choose an authentic, achievable project to pursue. Alternatively, connect with schools, libraries, town halls, and other community institutions to see whether you could join efforts in progress.

Related Texts

Water, Weed, and Wait
Written by Edith Hope Fine and
Angela Demos Halpin
Illustrated by Colleen Madden

Published by Tricycle Press (2010)
Grade Level: K-2

• • • • • • • •

Tell Me, Tree:
All about Trees for Kids (p.93)
Written and Illustrated by Gail
Gibbons

Published by Little Brown & Co.
(2002)
Grade Level: 1-4

• • • • • • • •

Our Community Garden
Written and Illustrated by
Barbara Pollak

Published by Beyond Words
Publishing (2003)
Grade Level: PreK-3

 **Lesson Plan**

Dichotomous Key

Objective	To understand plant identification basics by making a dichotomous key.

Time	1 hour

Materials	• Chalkboard or white board • Fruit and vegetable cards

Laying the Groundwork

Ask readers:

• Do you think gardeners know the identities of all plants? What are some ways to find out the names of plants we do not know? (Even very experienced gardeners do not know the names of all plants, so they use reference books and websites to identify unknown plants.)

• Why is it helpful to know a plant's identity? (Identification helps gardeners know what kind of conditions each plant needs so it can be planted in the right place.)

Exploration   1. Pass out the fruit and vegetable cards.
Ask readers to think of a way to divide the pictured fruits into two groups based on similar characteristics.

2. Continue to divide the groups again and again until the similarities are gone.

3. Show readers how the process of grouping by similarities and then distinguishing differences can lead to a dichotomous key. Here is an example:

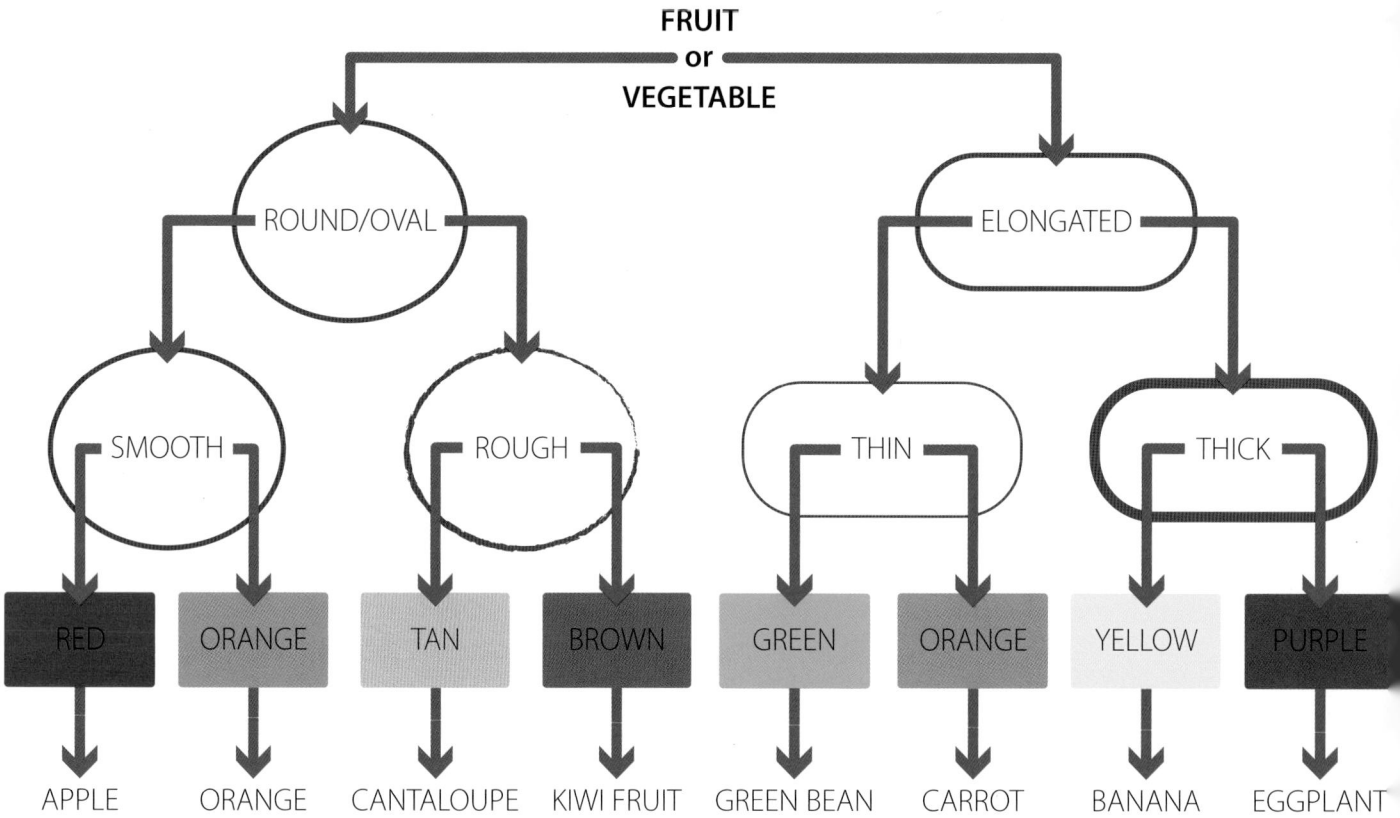

Branching Out   Test your identification skills in an outdoor space using a printed or online field guide (The Arbor Day Foundation has an online guide at *www.arborday.org/trees/whatTree/*).

APPLE

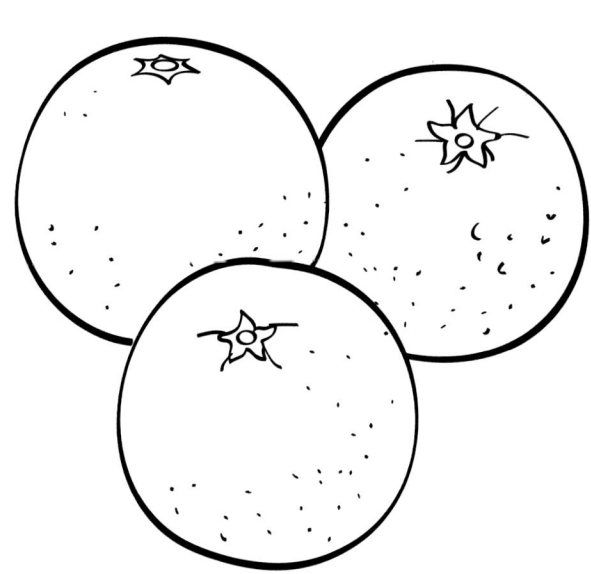

ORANGE

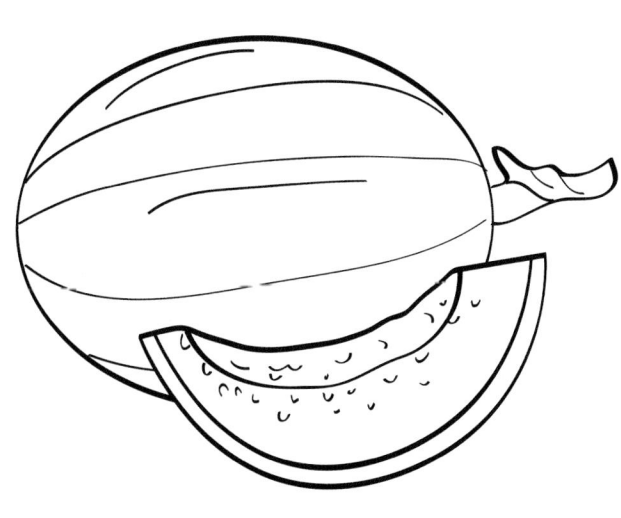

CANTALOUPE

KIWI FRUIT

GREEN BEAN

CARROT

BANANA

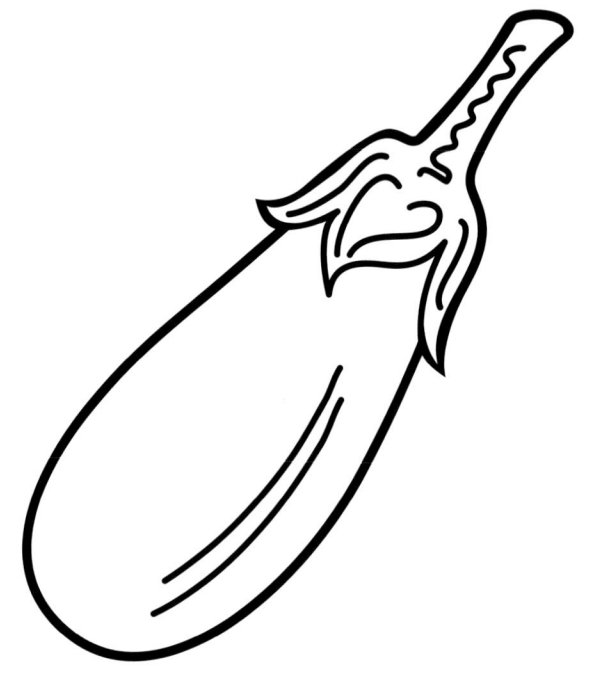

EGGPLANT

Plant Growth
Chart

118

Related Texts

There are many gardening books available for eager readers. If you can't get your hands on our featured texts, or your readers want more, try the suggestions below.

Featured Book	Related Book(s)	Similar Concept	Older Readers more advanced reading level	Younger Readers simpler reading level	Just for Fun
A Fruit is a Suitcase for Seeds	A Seed is Sleepy (Aston)	■			
Blueberries for Sal	Blueberries for the Queen (Paterson)				■
	Jamberry (Degen)				■
Compost Stew: An A-Z Recipe for the Earth	Water, Weed, and Wait (Fine & Halpin)	■			
	Diary of a Worm (Cronin)				■
Grandpa Green	Priscilla and the Hollyhocks (Broyles)		■		
	The Gardener (Stewart)	■			
In the Garden with Dr. Carver	First Garden: The White House Garden (Gourley)		■		
	Water, Weed, and Wait (Fine & Halpin)			■	
	Compost Stew: An A-Z Recipe for the Earth (Siddals)	■		■	
Jack's Garden	The Wind's Garden (Roberts)			■	
	The House I'll Build for the Wrens (Neitzel)				■
Miss Rumphius	The Wind's Garden (Roberts)			■	
	Planting the Wild Garden (Galbraith)	■			
	A Fruit is a Suitcase for Seeds (Richards)	■			
	The Plant Hunters: True Stories of Their Daring Adventures to the Far Corners of the Earth (Silvey)		■		■
Monarch and Milkweed	Monarch Butterfly (Gibbons)		■		
	An Extraordinary Life: The story of a Monarch Butterfly (Pringle)		■		
	Are you A Butterfly? (Allen & Humphries)	■		■	

Featured Book	Related Book(s)	Similar Concept	Older Readers (more advanced reading level)	Younger Readers (simpler reading level)	Just for Fun
Pick, Pull, Snap / Where Once a Flower Bloomed	Monarch and Milkweed (Frost)			■	
	The Reason for a Flower (Heller)			■	
Plant Secrets	A Seed is Sleepy (Aston)	■			
	A Fruit is a Suitcase for Seeds (Richards)	■			
Priscilla and the Hollyhocks	Klara's New World (Winter)			■	
	Miss Rumphius (Cooney)			■	
	Heart and Soul: The Story of America and African-Americans (Nelson)		■		
Pumpkin Circle: The Story of a Garden	A Fruit is a Suitcase for Seeds (Richards)	■			
	The Pumpkin Book (Gibbons)				■
	Pumpkin, Pumpkin (Titherington)			■	
Swirl by Swirl: Spirals in Nature	The Reason for a Flower (Heller)				■
Tell Me, Tree: All About Trees for Kids	Leaf Man (Ehlert)				■
The Gardener	Wanda's Roses (Brisson)	■			
	The Flower Garden (Bunting)			■	
	Stringbean's Trip to the Shining Sea (Wililams & Williams)				■
The Wind's Garden	A Fruit is a Suitcase for Seeds (Richards)	■	■		
	Dandelions, Stars in the grass (Posada)	■			
	Flip, Float, Fly: Seeds on the move (Macken)		■		
Wanda's Roses	Water, Weed, and Wait (Fine & Halpin)	■			
	Our Community Garden (Pollock)	■			
	Tell Me, Tree (Gibbons)				■

Common Core State Standards

English Language Arts and Literacy in History/Social Studies, Science, and Technical Subjects

The literature spotlighted in this book could be used to achieve any of the Common Core State Standards for English Language Arts and Literacy. Here is a list of possible connections using the lessons and activities suggested in Books in Bloom:

Featured Book	Suggested Grade Level	Literature CCSS.ELA-Literacy.RL.	Information Text CCSS.ELA-Literacy.RI.	Foundation Skills CCSS.ELA-Literacy.RF.	Writing Standards CCSS.ELA-Literacy.W.	Speaking and Listening Standards CCSS.ELA-Literacy.SL.	Language Standards CCSS.ELA-Literacy.L.
A Fruit is a Suitcase for Seeds	K–1	K-2.1 K-2.2 K-2.7	K-1.1 1.6 K-2.7			K-2.2 K-2.3	K-1.5
Blueberries for Sal	PreK–1	K-1.1 K-1.3 K-1.9				K-1.2 K.6	
Compost Stew: An A-Z Recipe for the Earth	K–4	K-4.1 K-3.7	K-4.1 K-4.2 K-1.3 4.5			K-4.2 K-4.4 K-2.5	
Grandpa Green	1–4	K-4.1 K-4.2 K-4.3 K-4.7			K-4.3	K-4.2 K-4.3 K-1.5	
In the Garden with Dr. Carver	2–5	2-5.1 2-5.3	2-5.1 2-5.2 2-5.3			2-5.1 2-5.2 2-5.3 2-5.4	
Jack's Garden	K–3	K-3.1 K-3.3 2.4 K-3.7	K-3.1 K-3.2 K-3.3 1-2.6 K-3.7	1-3.4	K-3.2	K-3-1 K-3.2 K-3.4	K-3.5
Miss Rumphius	K–3	K-2.1 K-2.3 K-2.7			1-2.7	K-2.1 K-2.2	
Monarch and Milkweed	K–3	K-3.1 K-3.7	K-3.1 K-3.2 K-3.3 K-3.7			K-3-1 K-3.2 K-1.5	

Featured Book	Suggested Grade Level (PreK, K, 1, 2, 3, 4, 5)	Literature CCSS.ELA-Literacy.RL	Information Text CCSS.ELA-Literacy.RI	Foundation Skills CCSS.ELA-Literacy.RF	Writing Standards CCSS.ELA-Literacy.W	Speaking and Listening Standards CCSS.ELA-Literacy.SL	Language Standards CCSS.ELA-Literacy.L
Pick, Pull, Snap / Where Once a Flower Bloomed	1, 2, 3, 4	1-4.1 / 1-4.7	1-4.1 / 1-4.2 / 2-4.3 / 1-4.7		1-4.2 / 1-4.6	1-4.1 / 1-4.2	
Plant Secrets	K, 1, 2	K-2.1 / 1-2.7	K-2.1 / K-2.2 / K-2.3 / K-2.7			K-2.1 / K-2.2 / K-2.3 / K-2.5	K-2.4 / K-2.5
Priscilla and the Hollyhocks	3, 4, 5	3-5.1 / 3-5.2 / 3-5.3	3-5.1 / 3-5.2 / 3-5.3 / 3-5.5 / 3-5.7	3.3	3-5.7 / 3-5.8	3-5.1 / 3-5.2 / 3-5.4	3-5.4
Pumpkin Circle: The Story of a Garden	K, 1, 2, 3, 4	K-4.1 / K-4.4 / K-4.7	K-4.1 / K-4.2 / K-4.3 / K-4.4 / 1-4.4 / K-4.7	K.2		K-4.1 / K-4.2 / K-4.5	1-4.1 / K-4.5
Swirl by Swirl: Spirals in Nature	K, 1, 2, 3	K-3.1 / K.4	K-3.1 / K-3.2 / K-3.3 / K-3.4 / 1-2.6 / K-3.7			K-3.1 / K-3.2 / K-3.3	1-3.1 / K-3.4 / K-3.5
Tell Me, Tree: All About Trees for Kids	1, 2, 3, 4	1-4.4	1-4.1 / 1-4.2 / 1-4.3 / 1-4.4 / 1-4.6 / 1-4.7		1-4.2 / 1-4.7 / 1-4.8	1-4.1 / 1-4.2	1-4.1 / 1-4.4
The Gardener	1, 2, 3	1-3.1 / 1-3.2 / 1-3.3 / 1-3.6 / 1-3.7 / 1.9			1-3.3 / 3.4	1-3.1 / 1-3.2 / 1-3.3 / 1-3.4	
The Wind's Garden	K, 1, 2	K-2.1 / K-2.7 / K-1.9	K-2.1 / K-2.2 / K-2.3 / 1-2.6 / K-2.7		K-2.8	K-2.1 / K-2.2 / K-2.3	
Wanda's Roses	K, 1, 2	K-2.1 / K-2.2 / K-2.3 / K-2.7 / K-1.9 / K10			1-2.7 / K-2.8	K-2.1 / K-2.2 / K-2.3 / K-2.4	

Next Generation Science Standards

The literature spotlighted in this book could be used to help achieve many performance expectations from the Next Generation Science Standards. Here is a list of the performance expectations that could be connected to the discussions, activities and lessons suggested in Books in Bloom:

Featured Book	Suggested Grade Level/Standards						
	Pre K	K	1	2	3	4	5
A Fruit is a Suitcase for Seeds		K-LS1-1 K-ESS3-1	1-LS1-2	2-LS2-2 2-LS4-1			
Blueberries for Sal		K-LS1-1 K-ESS3-1 K-ESS3-2					
Compost Stew: An A-Z Recipe for the Earth				2-PS1-1 2-PS1-2	3-LS1-1		
Grandpa Green						4-LS1-1	
In the Garden with Dr. Carver				2-PS1-1 2-PS1-2	3-LS1-1 3-LS3-2	4-ESS3-1	5-PS1-1 5-PS1-3 5-LS2-1
Jack's Garden		K-LS1-1 K-ES3-1	1-LS1-2	2-LS2-1 2-LS2-2 2-LS4-1	3-LS1-1		
Miss Rumphius		K-LS1-1 K-ESSE2-1 K-ESS3-1	1-LS1-2	2-LS2-2 2-LS4-1			
Monarch and Milkweed		K-LS1-1 K-ESS3-1		2-LS4-1	3-LS1-1 3-LS4-3 3-ESS2-2		
Pick, Pull, Snap Where Once a Flower Bloomed			1-LS1-2 1-ETS-1	2-LS2-2 2-LS4-1 2-ETS-1	3-LS1-1 3-LS3-1 3-LS3-2	4-LS1-1	
Plant Secrets		K-LS1-1 K-ESS3-1	1-LS1-2 1-LSE-1	2-LS2-2 2-LS4-1			
Priscilla and the Hollyhocks					3-LS1-1 3-LS4-3	4-LS1-1	
Pumpkin Circle: The Story of a Garden		K-LS1-1 L-ESS3-1	1-LS1-1 1-LS3-1	2-LS2-1	3-LS1-1 3-LS3-1 3-LS3-2	4-LS1-1	
Swirl by Swirl: Spirals in Nature		K-LS1-1 K-ETS-2	1-LS1-1 1-ETS-2	2-LS4-1 2-ETS-2			
Tell Me, Tree: All About Trees for Kids			1-LS3-1	2-PS1-1 2-LS2-1 2-LS4-1	3-LS1-1 3-LS3-2 3-ESS2-1	4-LS1-1	
The Gardener			1-LS3-1	2-LS2-1 2-LS4-1	3-LS3-2 3-LS4-3		
The Wind's Garden		K-LS1-1 K-ESS2-1	1-LS1-2	2-LS2-2 2-LS4-1			
Wanda's Roses		K-ESS3-1 K-ESS3-3	1-LS1-1	2-LS4-1			